THE MAN WHO SHOT J. P. MORGAN

TRUE CRIME HISTORY

The Man Who Shot J. P. Morgan: A Life of Arsenic, Anarchy, and Intrigue · Mary Noé
The Madness of John Terrell: Revenge and Insanity on Trial in the Heartland · Stephen Terrell
Queen of the Con: From a Spiritualist to the Carnegie Imposter · Thomas Crowl
The East River Ripper: The Mysterious 1891 Murder of Old Shakespeare · George R. Dekle Sr.
Cold War Secrets: A Vanished Professor, a Suspected Killer, and Hoover's FBI · Eileen Welsome
The Uncommon Case of Daniel Brown: How a White Police Officer Was Convicted of Killing a Black Citizen, Baltimore, 1875 · Gordon H. Shufelt
I Have Struck Mrs. Cochran with a Stake: Sleepwalking, Insanity, and the Trial of Abraham Prescott · Leslie Lambert Rounds
The Potato Masher Murder: Death at the Hands of a Jealous Husband · Gary Sosniecki
The Beauty Defense: Femmes Fatales on Trial · Laura James
Bigamy and Bloodshed: The Scandal of Emma Molloy and the Murder of Sarah Graham · Larry E. Wood
A Woman Condemned: The Tragic Case of Anna Antonio · James M. Greiner
Six Capsules: The Gilded Age Murder of Helen Potts · George R. Dekle Sr.
The Belle of Bedford Avenue: The Sensational Brooks-Burns Murder in Turn-of-the-Century New York · Virginia A. McConnell
The Insanity Defense and the Mad Murderess of Shaker Heights: Examining the Trial of Mariann Colby · William L. Tabac
Death of an Assassin: The True Story of the German Murderer Who Died Defending Robert E. Lee · Ann Marie Ackermann
The Lincoln Assassination Riddle: Revisiting the Crime of the Nineteenth Century · Edited by Frank J. Williams and Michael Burkhimer
Hauptmann's Ladder: A Step-by-Step Analysis of the Lindbergh Kidnapping · Richard T. Cahill Jr.
Nameless Indignities: Unraveling the Mystery of One of Illinois's Most Infamous Crimes · Susan Elmore
Guilty by Popular Demand: A True Story of Small-Town Injustice · Bill Osinski
The Supernatural Murders: Classic Stories of True Crime · Jonathan Goodman
The Christmas Murders: Classic Stories of True Crime · Jonathan Goodman
Murder and Martial Justice: Spying and Retribution in World War II America · Meredith Lentz Adams
Born to Lose: Stanley B. Hoss and the Crime Spree That Gripped a Nation · James G. Hollock
Queen Victoria's Stalker: The Strange Case of the Boy Jones · Jan Bondeson
The Adventuress: Murder, Blackmail, and Confidence Games in the Gilded Age · Virginia A. McConnell
Musical Mysteries: From Mozart to John Lennon · Albert Borowitz

The Man Who Shot J. P. Morgan

A LIFE OF ARSENIC, ANARCHY, AND INTRIGUE

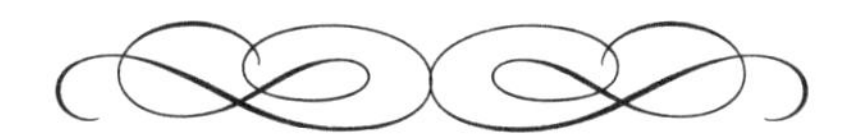

Mary Noé

The Kent State University Press *Kent, Ohio*

ISBN 978-1-60635-495-7
Published in the United States of America

Cataloging information for this title is available at the Library of Congress.

29 28 27 26 25 5 4 3 2 1

To my husband, the wind beneath my wings

CONTENTS

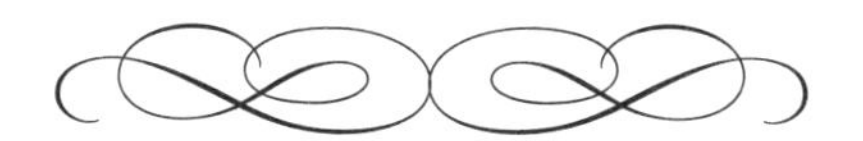

PART III. CREDITS NOT LOANS

PART IV. SEVEN DAYS IN JULY

ACKNOWLEDGMENTS

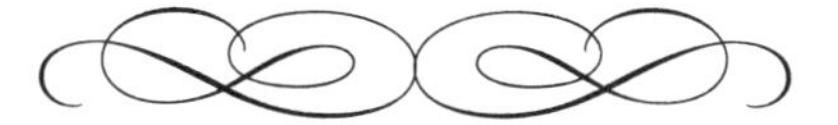

I am truly grateful for the support I received in what seemed at times like an insurmountable project. The people who have inspired and helped me along the way have gone above and beyond to read, critique, comment, and help make this book the best possible narrative nonfiction story.

One of my first daunting tasks was to secure information about Erich's first victim, his wife. The average woman at the turn of the century was mostly seen but not heard. How would I ever get to know a young woman of German descent who taught in Chicago schools in 1899? It's easy if you have her diary and letters. Steve Treanor, the Krembs family historian, invited me to the Krembs family reunion in 2019 at Steven's Point, Wisconsin. Steve has tirelessly supported me with information and kind words. He took me to the parking lot where relatives Bill and Alice MacDonald opened the hatchback of their car, and there was the treasure trove of her personal papers. I met the young victim who died in 1906 through her diary and letters. This find was only surpassed by reading her father's diary entry of the poisoning of the infant.

There are many books written about the bombastic J. Pierpont Morgan but just one about his quiet, unassuming son Jack Morgan. How fortunate I was to meet Jack's grandson, Robert Pennoyer, and talk with him about his grandfather. He was so kind and willingly read my manuscript. For five days we spoke on the phone going over the details about his grandfather and the Glen Cove estate. He was the consummate gentle man, a kind and generous soul. His daughter has been just as supportive as her father was to me.

I spent hours poring over hundreds of letters Jack wrote to his mother at the Morgan Library. The Morgan Library staff patiently provided me with his letters and writings, which gave me greater insight into the man behind the newspaper stories.

Friends and family read early drafts that needed overhauling, and their comments forced my hand to write more effectively. I am truly grateful for their input. They are scholars and professionals: P. Kevin Castel, Prof. Margaret Turano, and Patricia Skarulis. They are educated, wise, kind, patient friends and family: Ed Burne, Madelyn Fugazy, Joan Pisani, Arlene Radman, Joe Scott, Bill Sears, Louise Summers, Steve Treanor, and Gold Coast Librarian Richard Brower.

Libraries have always been one of my favorite places. I spent hours in the libraries in Chicago, Boston, Southern Methodist University, Cornell and Harvard universities. Librarians throughout the country have been a lifeline for me. This book would not exist without the librarians. Minute details that enrich a story were found in college and public libraries. The information transformed a chronology of events into a story. The Glen Cove Library Robert R. Cole's Historical Room allowed me to peruse their collection of Morgan documents. I am indebted to them all.

PROLOGUE

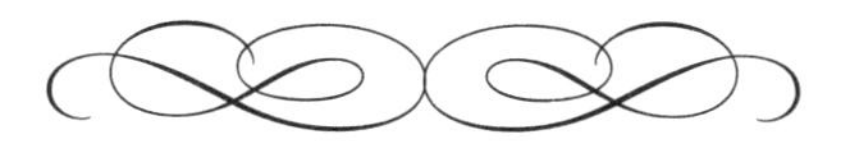

Society Summer Directory

Most of the world knew him as Mr. Morgan, the financier extraordinaire and reigning head of the House of Morgan, but his family and a small circle of confidants called him Jack.

On the morning of July 3, 1915, John Pierpont Morgan Jr. and his wife Jessie were enjoying the company of their house guests, the British ambassador Sir Cecil Spring Rice and his wife Florence, in the breakfast room of their summer estate on the Gold Coast of Long Island.

Within hours, the house would be filled with guests celebrating the honeymoon couple, Morgan's eldest son twenty-three-year-old Junius, and his bride, a Boston socialite.

This morning Jack and Jessie were able to relax in the style of a lord and lady who had entrusted the details to their exceedingly competent household staff.

The well-heeled would arrive in private cars passing the stately Pratt family manor homes along Dosoris Lane, then turning down a steep, winding road over a causeway and finally crossing the bridge onto East Island. Jack owned the island situated thirty miles east of Manhattan. He called his estate Matinicock. Locals, then and now, called it Morgan's Island. Guests attending the celebration would drive through an allée of linden trees on their way to the forty-one-room Georgian-style mansion.

Jack's 304-foot yacht, the *Corsair II,* with triple expansion steam engines providing for a smoother, faster-responding engine with minimal vibration, was docked on the west side of the island, alongside the *Navette,* the 114-foot steam yacht he used for commuting to Manhattan.

Every detail for the event had been planned with precision. The silver was polished, the crystal was washed and wiped until it all glistened, and the best English china adorned the tables. Jessie's prized delphiniums, called larkspur, cut from the island's gardens and hothouses, filled the vases. The menu *en français* had been prepared by the talented staff and approved by Mr. and Mrs. Morgan.

Sir Cecil made it his business to be well plugged in to influential Americans. More than a decade earlier, he served as best man at the London wedding of Teddy Roosevelt and his second wife Edith. While the British ambassador was happy to join in the Morgan family celebration, he could not completely block out the dire circumstances facing his country. The European War, ignited by the assassination of Archduke Ferdinand in Sarajevo, had erupted less than a year before. The war was taking a great toll on Britain and her Allies. The fighting, far from US shores, was on the minds of Americans. Jack had a keen interest because the war presented a grave threat to the House of Morgan and to the family real estate in London and Paris.

Neither Sir Cecil nor Jack was a fan of the Wilson administration's policy of strict neutrality in the war. But by late 1914, a reluctant Wilson administration was persuaded to draw a distinction between direct "loans" to belligerents and trade "credits" available for use in making purchases from American companies. This allowed Morgan & Co. to extend "credits" to Britain and France—at a suitable interest rate—to finance purchases of munitions and supplies from American vendors. By the summer of 1915, the Morgan firm had already provided millions in credit to Britain. But Britain needed more. The May 7 sinking of Britain's Lusitania by a German U-boat was the latest atrocity of the war.

On this cool Saturday morning, Sir Cecil, his wife, and the Morgans sat peacefully sipping tea and coffee while enjoying the breathtaking views of the Sound.

At nine-thirty in the morning the doorbell rang. Cecil Physick, the properly attired thirty-six-year-old butler, was available to greet the unexpected early morning guests. When Cecil opened the door, a six-foot-tall, thin man dressed in a blue serge jacket appeared and said, "I want to see Mr. Morgan." The visitor then handed Physick his card, which read, "Society Summer Directory. Represented by Thomas C. Lester."

Within seconds after Physick refused his entry, the steel barrels of two revolvers pressed against his ribs.

Part I

Leone Krembs

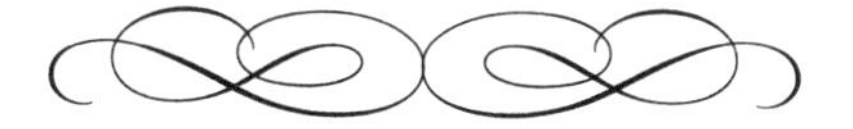

I only knew what hunted thought
Quickened his step, and why
He looked upon the garish day
With such a wistful eye;
The man had killed the thing he loved,
And so he had to die.

OSCAR WILDE, *THE BALLAD OF READING GAOL*, 1898

CHAPTER 1

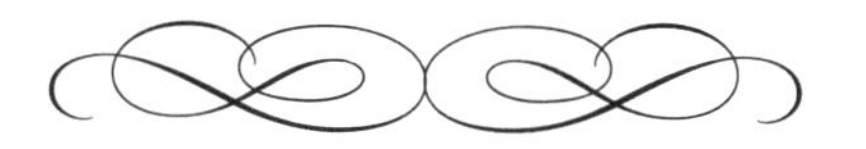

It's All Over

Nine years before, in the cool early morning hours of April 16, 1906, at 107 Oxford Street, Cambridge, Massachusetts, Erich Muenter quietly approached the dining room of his apartment where Mrs. Edith Chase was sleeping. He tapped on the door. Mrs. Edith Chase, a self-claimed Christian Science nurse, had been hired to attend to his wife during childbirth. She jumped up from the cot and was relieved she didn't wake the ten-day-old infant beside her. When she opened the door, she saw Erich's vacant stare.

"It's all over," he said.

Mrs. Chase asked, "What's over?"

"It's all over. My wife is dead."[1]

Mrs. Chase ran into the bedroom and saw the young mother's body. Her eyes were partially open, and her peach-colored skin had the hint of yellow—or was it blue? There was a putrid smell. Mrs. Chase could not understand how it was possible that there had not been a sound from her passing. "What time did she die?"[2]

Erich said he fell asleep at Leone's bedside and awoke around six in the morning to find her lifeless. As soon as Mrs. Chase saw Leone's rigid body, she knew she had been dead for quite some time. Rigor mortis had set in.

Weeks before, Leone and Mrs. Chase had agreed on the course of her prenatal and postnatal care. Mrs. Chase claimed, as a member of the Church of Christ, Scientist, to abide by their "medical system." Believers accepted that illness was an idea of the mind. The "readers" conducted the weekly worship services, while the "practitioners" had the ministry of spiritual healing, which included inaudible prayers in the presence of the patient or, at times, delivered from miles away. Medical intervention was prohibited. The church's following had grown exponentially since Mary Baker Eddy founded the religion in 1879. Three miles from Erich and Leone's apartment in Boston was the Christian Science's "Mother Church." In 1906 it was still under construction and the *Boston Globe* described it as the "largest, most expensive and most magnificent religious edifice in New England," with a "dome higher than Bunker Hill Monument" and a "mile and a half [of] mahogany of pews, with seats for 5,000."[3] The reported cost in 1906 was $2 million ($69 million in 2024).

It had only been ten days since Leone gave birth to a healthy baby girl. Now she was dead.

Leone's death was tragic but not shocking. Her steady decline started two days following childbirth. Maternal deaths were infrequent but not unknown. In 1905 Massachusetts reported 75,000 births and 318 deaths occurring in women in the puerperal state, or postpartum, primarily categorized as "sudden death" and "blood poisoning" from a bacterial infection.

The unnamed newborn's wailing broke the silence in the apartment. She needed to be cleaned and fed. Her three-year-old sister, Helen, awoke from the infant's wailing only to join in the crying. Disjointed thoughts raced through Erich's mind—the loss of his wife, the care of a newborn and a toddler, burial and cemetery expenses, and possibly an uncertain, dark future.

Erich called St. Auburn Cemetery, located blocks away, to arrange for the cremation of Leone's body. Auburn provided a list of required documents. A death certificate was required. He did not have one.

Erich immediately called a reluctant Dr. McIntire and persuaded him to return to the apartment. Erich had previously contacted McIntire requesting a house call before and after childbirth. Leone was in distress due to a stomach ailment. Each time the doctor visited, he was presented with a conundrum. Erich described his wife's adherence to Christian Science and her stated intention to decline medical treatment. But unlike his wife, Erich expressed an understanding and appreciation of the benefits of medicine. McIntire would examine Leone and prescribe medication. When he learned his directives were not followed, he discontinued his services. On his return visit, Erich reassured him that he was not the obstacle to medical treatment. Erich was well-educated, a scholar, who respected the medical profession and if he could, would have followed the doctor's advice.

On this day, Erich brought McIntire to the room where Leone's body lay motionless. McIntire looked at the young mother and perhaps pulled back the cover to see her body wasted and emaciated in the bed. He could not determine the cause of death. Erich implored him to sign the death certificate so that he could lay his beloved wife to rest. McIntire knew from his last visit that Erich's wife had been gravely ill. Erich reasoned with the doctor who he felt had sufficient reasons to sign off on a death certificate. Common decency and the respect for a grieving spouse, the father of two children and a respected Harvard man, demanded no less. McIntire listened to Erich's plea but felt no obligation to sign the death certificate. He likely regretted his return. McIntire's resolve strengthened, and he left the home having signed nothing.

When McIntire returned to his office, he called the medical examiner of Middlesex County.

The next call Erich made was to a local undertaker, George W. Long. Eager for new business, Long left at once for the Muenter home. Long was met at the door by Erich, who appeared to Long to be a distinguished, fine-looking man about thirty-five years old, slight of build, about five foot eleven, with a thick, dark head of hair and neatly trimmed beard. He escorted Long into the apartment. Long noticed Erich's disjointed gait. Erich took Long to the bedroom and requested that he transport the body to St. Auburn Cemetery. Long observed Leone's body was unusually contorted. He asked Erich for the death certificate. Erich, without mentioning Dr. McIntire, told Long that Dr. Taylor, who had also visited Leone, would sign the death certificate.

Long would later say that Erich was confused as to whether he wanted the body embalmed and then transferred or taken directly to the crematorium, but Long remembered that the man was anxious to get the body removed from the apartment. Embalming was unnecessary if the body was to be cremated. Long was sympathetic, but his lifetime of experience counseled caution. He would not rely on the widower's word that later Dr. Taylor would sign a death certificate. Long refused to embalm or transport the body without a death certificate.

Out of compassion for the widower or, perhaps to preserve his reputation in the community, Long cleaned the bed of fluids, washed and dressed Leone's thin, withered body, then carefully placed it back on the bed. He closed the young mother's eyes and placed a pillow under her head so she would appear to be sleeping.

Long was haunted by what he had seen. Upon returning to his office, Long called the medical examiner.

Erich, now down to his last option, contacted Dr. Taylor. He, too, had terminated his care of the patient because his medical advice had not been followed. Dr. Taylor returned to the apartment, saw Leone's body, and abruptly left without signing a death certificate. Unknown to Erich, the medical examiner received a third call.

It became clear to Erich that he needed a death certificate to transport Leone's body to her final resting place. But time and options were running out.

CHAPTER 2

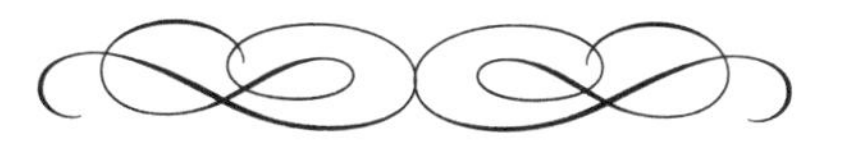

Gastro-duodenitis

The postpartum death of Mrs. Erich Muenter raised nothing more than rank suspicion. Dr. William D. Swan, the Middlesex County medical examiner, had received three telephone calls on Monday morning, April 16, following the death of the young mother. Dr. McIntire and Dr. Taylor reported details from their examinations, treatment, and follow-up during her final illness. Nothing was straightforward. The husband was a Harvard PhD candidate and a respected instructor of philology, the study of language in classical literature. He enjoyed a fine reputation among his academic colleagues and the community at large. Reportedly, his wife, the decedent, had been devout in her religious beliefs and opposed to medical treatment.

Without the benefit of a treating physician's judgment on the matter, it was now left to Dr. Swan to determine the cause and manner of the unexplained death posthaste. A forensic autopsy would be necessary. He needed to prepare a report with his findings based on his autopsy, laboratory reports, and any information received from previously attending physicians. If there was probable evidence of a crime, Dr. Swan could be called as a witness at a legal proceeding, such as an inquest, a grand jury investigation, or a trial.

Dr. William Donnison Swan's credentials exceeded those of other county medical examiners. He was a graduate of Harvard Medical

School whose postgraduate program included rotations at hospitals in Boston and Vienna. The then newly elected governor of Massachusetts, William E. Russell, appointed Swan to be the medical examiner of Middlesex County after only three years in private practice. Swan was now in his fifteenth year as ME.

Swan's reputation as an ME was solid. A month before the death of Leone Muenter, Dr. Swan had been summoned to a ravine where a young woman's severed head was found. He became the key witness at the murder trial. Over the defense counsel's objection, Swan produced a bone from the woman's skull and testified that it had the imprint of a knife blade. The defendant's fate was sealed.

Standard procedure dictated that the ME needed two other physicians to attend an autopsy. Swan asked McIntire and Taylor to accompany him to the Muenter residence. Taylor demurred but McIntire agreed. Swan then requested Dr. Thomas M. Durrell, a Harvard man and the medical examiner of the City of Somerville, to complete the trio.

When the three arrived at the Muenter home in the afternoon at 2:30, Erich recognized Dr. McIntire. Dr. Swan identified himself as the medical examiner and introduced Dr. Durrell. Swan explained to Professor Muenter that because his wife had died at home and had no "treating" physician, it was his responsibility to determine the cause of death. Only then could he complete a death certificate. In order to make the determination, he needed to perform an autopsy. "Autopsy" was a trigger word to the grieving Erich. He became agitated, indignant, and irritated. The three physicians were an imposing presence in his home. He sensed that these doctors were unfazed and unimpressed by his intellect, integrity, and reputation.

Each time Dr. McIntyre and Dr. Taylor treated Leone, Erich provided detailed information about Leone's adherence to the teachings of Christian Science. He now begrudgingly found himself repeating his wife's sincerely held beliefs to this team of doctors.

Swan and Durrell listened patiently even though they had been briefed by McIntire on the situation. McIntire's patience had grown thin listening to the iterations Erich had provided to him on each visit.

Swan insisted on an autopsy. Erich refused to allow it. He told the trio that Leone had spoken to him many times about death and her wishes. Did they not understand that she wanted no medical interference? Erich tried to cajole them. He described his wife's desire that her body never be mutilated in life or death. Were they so unreasonable as to not honor the young mother's dying request?

Erich added another reason: Leone's family would never approve of such a barbaric procedure. The doctors listened impassively and with feigned interest. It was a scene that Swan had experienced many times before as the ME. Swan patiently laid out an ultimatum—he could perform a minimally invasive procedure now in the apartment or else the body would be removed to the morgue, where an autopsy would be performed. There were no other options.

The next clash of wills escalated when Swan told Erich he had to remain outside the bedroom during the autopsy and that the door would be closed. This further enraged the frenetic professor, but Swan was experienced in handling difficult people.

Once in the bedroom, Swan took charge and the other doctors assisted. Swan's black bag contained medical tools not carried by treating physicians. There were forceps, scissors, and a surgical razor, the forerunner of the present-day scalpel.

The doctors examined the body. Immediately, the three recognized that a significant amount of time had lapsed between Leone's death and their procedure. Perhaps they saw the small blisters that covered her skin like the sheen on a three-day-old dead fish or smelled a garlic odor. Each doctor was thoroughly familiar with the postpartum female condition. When they removed Leone's clothing, they noticed abnormalities, notably her distended, swollen abdomen, which was inconsistent with her recent childbirth. Swan's exceptional experience caused him to focus on opening Leone's abdomen, and he made incisions so that her abdominal organs could be examined. The incisions caused no bleeding because there was no pumping heart.

With every cut, Erich's footsteps outside the door grew louder, back and forth, like those of a caged tiger. His audible muttering was distracting. There were repeated chants about his wife's spirit, her family, and her religious beliefs.

The doctors proceeded with a sense of urgency to finish lest he burst into the room.

When the gastrointestinal organs were exposed, they appeared enlarged and inflamed. Swan's years of experience gave him reason to suspect a cause, but he spoke not a word. Swan knew he needed to excise the organs, specifically the liver, and take them without Erich's knowledge. They were wrapped in cloth and carefully placed in his black bag. The clasp of the bag was secured shut. The doctors quickly sewed up the abdomen, cleaned the area, dressed Leone, reclaimed the surgical instruments, and in a flash left the room.

Swan had previously removed a blank death certificate from his bag so as not to open it in Erich's presence. The words "cause of death" glared at him. There was little time to ruminate over the answer. The first part of the small intestine was grossly enlarged. With a stroke of his pen he wrote "Gastro-duodenitis,"[1] meaning nothing more than an enlarged small intestine. Swan and the attending doctors agreed that the date of death was April 15, not April 16, as reported by Erich. He handed the death certificate to Erich without him noticing the date of death. Then the doctors rushed out of the apartment.

Swan immediately contacted Dr. William Fiske Whitney, first surgical pathologist of Massachusetts General Hospital, curator of the Warren Anatomical Museum at Harvard Medical School, and dean emeritus of the same institution, to which J. Pierpont Morgan was a major benefactor. Whitney was eminently qualified to test the organs. Whitney's report would not be available for several weeks. Swan would personally deliver Leone's organs to Whitney.

Swan took one more step that was not customary for most autopsies. He telephoned Capt. Patrick J. Hurley, chief inspector of the Cambridge Police Department. The Cambridge police needed to wait for Whitney's report. The delay caused a missed opportunity to question Erich, which would not occur again for years.

CHAPTER 3

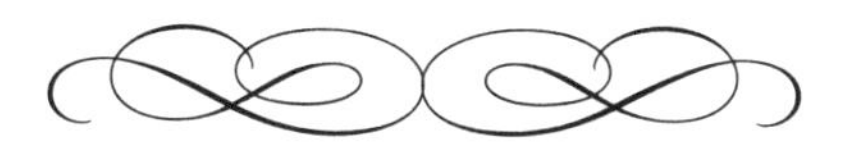

Going Home

The day after the baby's birth Leone wrote to her father Moritz Krembs. His diary entry captured his daughter's elation and relief: "Received eleven-page long letter from Leone, written on the 7th. Felt very strong and happy."[1]

But soon after the news began to change. A few days later her parents received a postcard from Erich describing Leone's deteriorating condition. Erich urged Moritz and Johanna Krembs not to be alarmed. He assured them her illness was not serious and she would be well soon.

Moritz's experience as a pharmacist, chemist, and thirty-year member of the Chicago Veteran Druggist Association alerted him to several serious conditions that his daughter might have. But he could do nothing. He lived over nine hundred miles away.

Erich needed to summon the courage to call her family and tell them of her demise. The Krembs family was close-knit. Leone previously spent only one year away from her parents and siblings when Erich was teaching at the University of Kansas in 1903.

Leone, at twenty-nine years old, fell for the handsome, charismatic, intelligent young man who tutored her during her teacher's training at Chicago's Normal School. Within a year, the couple spoke of marriage. Leone's parents disapproved because Erich's prospects were uncertain. They would reconsider if Erich completed his graduate education and became fully employed. This request fell on deaf ears. Despite parental disapproval, the couple married at the Christian People's Church.

Eleven months later Helen was born. One year after Helen's birth, Erich suddenly abandoned his graduate studies at the University of Chicago. He had been working on his thesis, "Insanity in German Romantic Literature." He also quit his teaching positions at Racine College and Kenwood Preparatory School and decided to uproot Leone and their baby. He landed a position as an instructor for the school year 1903–4 at the University of Kansas in Lawrence by falsely claiming that he had a PhD from the University of Chicago.

Leone's letters to her family describe her angst over finances: "Erich just had his check cashed and he says this is as much as he can spare this month, but will send the $30 plus extras I owe you as soon as the next salary come in. . . . Rents and living are as high here as in Chicago. Erich was refused rooms at many, almost all places when he informed them of having a baby."[2]

The next academic year, Erich received the news he longed for. He had been accepted as a PhD student in philology and offered a position as an instructor at an academic institution worthy of his talents, Harvard. In his application to Harvard, Erich wrote, "I am married. My wife and baby will stay with relatives in Chicago next year and will be depending upon me for support but to a very limited extent."[3] It was impossible to support a family of three in Cambridge. Leone and Helen returned to Chicago, where she was now able to work again as a teacher.

In July 1905, Leone and Helen arrived in Cambridge. Leone believed they would summer with Erich, and then she and Helen would return to Chicago during the school year and resume teaching. Erich had a different plan. Leone wrote her sister:

> Dearest Louise, I believe Louise, I am *going to have* to stay. Only to-day Erich settled down to a talk on the subject, tho from the very first, he referred to our staying as a matter of fact."
> Yours lovingly, Leone[4]

Three-year-old Helen, unaccustomed to life in Cambridge with her father, whined for her grandmother: "Nach Hause gehen—nach Omama (go home—go Grandma)."[5] Helen repeated her protests. Leone reported to her sister that "Erich took her to the bathroom to discipline her."[6]

Louise could not imagine Christmas "with out dear little Helen. A kiss for Helen from each & love from each for you all."[7]

Louise had been critical of Erich's treatment of Leone, writing to her four months before her death, "My very, very dear, quite neglected sister."[8]

One month after Leone's arrival she was pregnant. She had no other option but to remain in Cambridge. She expressed delight at the prospect of a second child, prepared a layette, and received a catalog for infant outfits from Best & Co. on New York's Fifth Avenue. She sewed bibs and slips with her newly purchased Singer sewing machine. Her prior pregnancy and birth were uneventful and she expected this to be the same.

Erich reached a long-distance operator and placed a call to his father-in-law. There was no way to soften the blow. He knew that news of her death would shock and devastate the family. Erich told Moritz that Leone died on April 16. He furnished his own cause of death, a blood disorder. He added details of his attempts to provide medical treatment for her, but she had refused because of her Christian Science faith. Erich told his father-in-law that he had made plans with St. Auburn Cemetery to have Leone's body cremated, which were Leone's wishes.

Moritz was stunned. Despite his state of shock and confusion, he directed Erich to bring Leone and her babies back home to Chicago. There would be no cremation in Cambridge. He would not allow his daughter to be buried so far from home. On that point, he was resolute.

Honoring this request upended Erich's plans and presented a new set of problems. He needed to have Leone's body embalmed for the arduous trip to Chicago. How would he manage traveling by train for twenty-plus hours with his three-year-old daughter and a ten-day-old infant? Moritz had once again imposed an unfair and unnecessary burden on him.

There was an additional responsibility. Erich needed to return to Cambridge to resume his classes after the Easter recess. He had not informed anyone at Harvard that his wife had died.

In the morass, he took just a moment to wire the sad news to his longtime friend and former teaching colleague at the University High School in Chicago, John Maxwell Crowe: "Prof. Crowe, Chicago, Ill. April 17, 1906. I am bringing my dear one to Chicago. Leone died. Helen and the baby are well. Erich Muenter."[9]

If there had to be a trip to Chicago, it needed to be done quickly for the sake of everyone. He studied the train schedule, called the undertaker, and told him to come over as soon as possible. He now had a death certificate, and he, the children, and Leone's body had to be on the two o'clock train to Chicago.

Long and his son immediately went to the Oxford Street home. Leone had been dead for over forty-eight hours. Long had his work cut out for him since he would need to comply with Massachusetts State Board of Registration in Embalming for the Transportation of the Dead. All cavities needed to be filled "with an approved disinfectant,"[10] all orifices stopped with absorbent cotton, and the entire body covered with one inch-cotton, then wrapped in a sheet and bandaged, and "encased in an air-tight coffin or casket."[11]

In the immediate aftermath of Leone's death, Erich and Mrs. Chase cared for the children. Now Erich informed Mrs. Chase that he was leaving for Chicago and asked her to accompany him. He offered to cover all her expenses for the trip. She declined.

It would be impossible for Erich to travel thirty to forty hours to Chicago and care for his daughter and a newborn. Although he was an exceptional scholar and worked obsessively when teaching and tutoring, he could not handle a toddler and a few days-old newborn on a long trip.

Since Leone's death, the Muenter apartment on Oxford Street had seen more activity than ever before. The neighbors heard of the new mother's death after the birth of her daughter. In prior months, they had seen Leone with three-year-old Helen. She was friendly but quiet and kept mostly to herself. At 11:30 on the morning of April 17, some of the neighbors arrived at the Muenter apartment to pay condolences to the mild-mannered professor.

One neighbor, Mrs. Bertha Derrick, a nurse, found the grief-stricken husband overwhelmed with the care of the children. A sympathetic person of generous spirit, she volunteered to help. It had been her understanding that Leone's body was to be cremated at St. Auburn Cemetery in Cambridge. She was startled when Erich told her that he, the children, and Leone's body were leaving for Chicago in a few hours. Mrs. Derrick, out of sympathy, agreed to accompany the family.

Erich hurriedly packed clothes and necessities for himself, the three-year-old, and the unnamed newborn. Despite the need to move expeditiously, he would lug his trunk of papers to Chicago. His plan was to return to Cambridge after the burial and a suitable family collation.

The coffin was borne by the undertaker George Long and his son, in a horse-drawn wagon.

Erich contacted Theodore W. Hiller, a neighbor, who lived in the same house to drive the family and Bertha Derrick to the train station. Erich had a cordial relationship with Ted and often spoke to him about the new experimental language he had been formulating since his college days at the University of Chicago, a mix of Scottish and broad German. Ted, who was not an academic, found Erich's language idea bizarre, typical of a head-in-the-clouds Harvard scholar.

Hiller drove Erich and his entourage to Boston's South Station, one of the world's largest train stations. The station flaunted a granite eight-foot wingspan eagle perched on top of the building's cupola. Minutes after their arrival, the monumental station's clock would strike two o'clock.

Erich was clearly anxious, pacing the station's platform and nagging a trainman with questions about departure and arrival train times. After the coffin was loaded onto the funeral car, Erich, wearing his coat and customary derby, walked over to Mr. Long, thanking him for all that he had done. From his pocket, Erich drew a large wad of bills and offered to pay Long's expenses. Long, observing the roll of money, protested and insisted that Erich pay when he returned from the Midwest. Erich ignored Long's protestations and peeled off some ten-dollar bills and handed them to Long. It was the only money he would receive from Erich.

The group boarded the New York Central Railroad's train to Chicago. They traveled through the night. In the early light of the morning, two thousand miles further west, an earthquake was devastating the city of San Francisco. News buzzed across the wires but was out of reach of the train. Erich was melancholic and grief-stricken over his own miseries. He hardly spoke to Mrs. Derrick. He seemed to carry the weight of the world on his shoulders. He only responded to mundane inquiries of the train conductor.

Erich was returning to the couple's hometown with his children and a coffin. Waiting for him would be a bombardment of questions from Leone's family.

CHAPTER 4

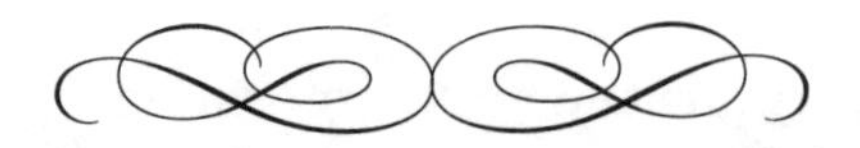

Leone's Spirit

Seventeen thousand travelers a day passed through Chicago's Grand Central Station. Moritz, his wife, Johanna, and their daughter Louise anxiously waited in the throng. Crowds of passengers with porters moving their luggage and belongings crisscrossed paths and filled the vast building. Train traffic destined for San Francisco was halted because the earthquake caused railroads to collapse along with buildings. There were fires and no water to extinguish them.

The Krembs waited inside the station adorned with marble floors, twenty-six-foot-high ceilings, Corinthian columns, stained-glass windows, and a marble fireplace.

The striking of the 11,000-pound bell ringing in the 247-foot tower alerted the Krembs to the hour that the train carrying their family would arrive. Through the screeching of brakes, bursts of steam, and the odor of burning coal, the Krembs scanned the faces of the travelers. The Muenter entourage appeared in the crowd. The grandparents spotted Helen with Erich and a swaddled infant in a stranger's arms. What might have been an elated greeting for a newborn was instead a sharp, painful reminder that their daughter was dead. There would be no happy reunion for the grieving Krembs family. It was somber and mournful except for the obligatory fuss over Helen and the newborn.

After meeting up with the Krembs family at Grand Central Station, the widower, children, and the altruistic Mrs. Derrick traveled with the Krembs to their home at 479 Fullerton Avenue. Bertha Derrick would later describe the home as one for the well-to-do.

Moritz worked hard to provide for his family. He did his part to fulfill the dream of his parents, who had ten children and had fled Prussia in 1848 at the onset of the German revolution. The Krembs settled in the German immigrant community of Fond du Lac, Wisconsin. Moritz came from a family with a strong work ethic. His father served as a pharmacist to the German royal family before the revolution and Moritz followed his profession. He married Johanna, a German immigrant from New York. Leone, born in 1871, was the fourth of their seven surviving children.

Moritz then moved to Chicago because he sensed there were greater opportunities there. Oscar Mayer, from Württemberg, Germany, started his butcher shop there at the age of twenty-four. Julius Rosenwald, a Bavarian immigrant, guided the early expansion and growth of Sears-Roebuck in Chicago. Ignaz Schwinn, a German-born mechanical engineer, created his own brand of bicycles. The Hart brothers opened a men's clothing store on State Street, later called Hart, Schaffner and Marx.

Moritz purchased a drugstore on West Randolph Street, a few blocks from the "wild carnage" of the 1886 Haymarket riots arising from a bombing at an otherwise peaceful protest by striking workers employed by the McCormick International Harvester Company demanding better hours, wages, and conditions.

Moritz and Johanna Krembs's rented their home, which stands today as it did in 1906, with a Victorian wood-paneled foyer, seven-foot mirror, doors opening to a large living and dining room featuring ten-foot ceilings. The staircase was adorned with a carved wooden banister and each room with handsome moldings on the walls and door frames. The home was situated at the end of a row-house block owned by the McCormick Theological Seminary, a Presbyterian institution headquartered in Indiana. The benefactor of the seminary was Cyrus McCormick, who founded his harvesting company, which was the same company at the center of the Haymarket riots.

The Krembs home had been so full of family and love for the young Leone, who grew up in the warm embrace of her parents and siblings. She excelled in school, enjoyed German traditions, and visited the Columbian Exposition in 1893. "[The] sweet sounds of music wafted on the evening breezes . . . And [there was] the thrill of the ride of 'two revolutions' on the Ferris wheel."[1]

Her chaperoned nighttime visits to the Exposition were exhilarating. She could see from blocks away the glow of 200,000 electric lights, powered by a new form of energy. She loved the nostalgia of the German beer gardens and delighted in the performances of Buffalo Bill Cody and his sharpshooting cowboys. The Exposition was filled with displays of new tasty treats like the caramel-covered popcorn, later called Cracker Jack, introduced by the German immigrant Louis Ruckheim, Juicy Fruit chewing gum developed by William Wrigley Jr., and the chocolate of Milton Hershey, of Swiss and German descent. One item displayed at the Exposition featured the image of a formerly enslaved woman Nancy Green on a box of Aunt Jemima's Pancake Flour. The Krembs family was filled with pride when Moritz was permitted to display at the Exposition his chicory from his farm in Racine.

Now a pall hung over the home.

Leone's brothers, thirty-three-year-old Walter, and twenty-six-year-old Eugene, seethed. They were not intimidated by the Harvard scholar, nor would they let the solemnity of the day interfere with their quest for answers.

Erich found Leone's family to be suffocating.

Erich's family, who also settled in Chicago, had not been as successful. His father, Ernest, a German merchant, died in 1893, four years after arriving in the United States, Erich, then twenty-one years old, assumed responsibility for his mother and three sisters.

Erich told Leone's family that he and Leone both agreed to be cremated in the event of death and now he wanted to carry out their mutual wishes. Both, he said, feared being buried alive. "She must be cremated, for her soul will go away with the smoke and will not be left in the ashes. If she is buried, her spirit will remain on earth to come before me and torture me."[2] His choice of words was beyond strange. Perhaps his grief rendered him incoherent.

No member of the Krembs family had ever been cremated. Emotionally unprepared for Leone's death, the family members were at odds with her husband's request. Whether the family accepted Erich's story at this point is unknown, but Moritz took charge and decided to oblige the grieving husband's request to cremate and then bury her ashes. Moritz described Erich as being in a terrible state, vacillating between morose and irrational. Leone's brothers, Walter and Eugene, found Erich peculiar and were insistent on getting answers. How did she die? Who was present? Did Erich call a doctor? They cornered Erich, who refused to answer their questions, put his face in his hands, and cried that his mind was confused and he was unable to think.

CHAPTER 5

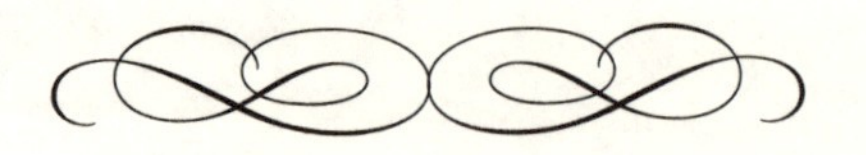

Money

Moritz Krembs placed a terse death notice in the *Chicago Tribune:* "MUENTER—Leone Muenter, nee Krembs, beloved wife of Erich Muenter, in Boston, Mass., April 16. Funeral Thursday at 2 P.M. 479 E. Fullerton Ave."[1]

Moritz restated the only information Erich provided about his daughter's date of death.

Leone's mother asked Bertha Derrick, the Cambridge neighbor, to stay at their home for several days. The tearful scene could not have been very enticing. Bertha declined and returned to Boston on the morning train. That evening, Erich stayed at his sister Agnes's apartment along with his sister Bertha. Erich's mother Julia and sister Louise were living in California. Helen and the newborn remained with the Krembs family.

The next morning, when Erich returned to the Krembs's home, he found a procession of family and friends extending their condolences. Some of Leone's fellow teachers from the Schiller School came and spoke fondly of their departed friend. The principal of the school sent a sympathy note. Leone had returned to work in 1904 after Helen's birth and a mandatory two-year postpartum furlough.

It seemed the news of Leone's death spread quickly in the close-knit German American community. Erich would repeat that she died of complications from childbirth, a blood disorder that was untreated because of her commitment to the tenets of Christian Science.

Walter and Eugene pressed Erich for more information. The stoic widower's stress level was elevated. Erich said he went to bed at three in the morning on April 16, and when he checked on Leone at six in the morning, she was dead, a time line different from one told to Edith Chase. Leone's brothers were unaware that the medical examiner had set the date of death as April 15. In an attempt to quench Leone's brothers' insatiable thirst for details, Erich slipped his hand in the pocket of his jacket and removed a note and handed it to Walter and Eugene. The note was in Erich's handwriting followed by the signature of their dead sister. It said she refused any medical intervention should it be needed, and if she should die, Erich would be released from any responsibility.

Walter and Eugene's anger was palpable after they read the note. Instead of satisfying their quest for information, the note did the opposite. Did their sister sign this note in her dying days when she was unable to write it herself? Wasn't this evidence that Erich predicted Leone's death and he was attempting to vindicate himself? Did Erich think that they were such fools as to accept the note as an exoneration? Now they fired more pointed questions. Why did Erich need a written exculpation from his dying wife? What happened to their sister after childbirth? Erich's answers were incoherent.

Leone's brothers were convinced their sister died at the hand of Erich. They had a deep-seated distrust of him years before when Leone gave birth to Helen. Now that incident was foremost on their minds.

About four years earlier, Erich and Leone shared their first apartment in Chicago with Erich's colleague at the University High School, John Maxwell Crowe and his wife. This was the same John Crowe whom Erich alerted about his return to Chicago after Leone died. Erich and Leone had lived in the front rooms of the apartment and Crowe and his wife in the back. The apartment was equipped with gas lamps, which could light up a room with the turn of a knob and the strike of a match. Some landlords converted to electric lights after the Exposition but many apartments continued to use gas lamps.

Leone was recuperating in the days after giving birth to Helen. One afternoon, Erich and Crowe were sitting outside the apartment, most likely discussing their scholarly pursuits. Suddenly, a hysterical neighbor ran out of her apartment, screaming for help. She detected the smell of gas. It was coming from the Muenter apartment. The gas lamps on the wall of Leone's room were in the open position without a flame. Gas was filling the room. The bedroom windows and door were closed, yet the gas had seeped into a neighbor's apartment. It would not have taken long for Leone to become unconscious.

Crowe denied Leone's brothers' second-hand version of the story but declined to furnish his own account. Leone's brothers were convinced that Erich had turned on all the gas jets without lighting them while Leone was asleep. He then shut the windows and doors and left.

Years later Walter made a keen observation. "He [Erich] didn't say why the gas was needed in a well-lit room in the middle of the afternoon and why three jets should have been turned on at once, and why all of them should have been unlighted—but we accepted his explanation"[2] or so they said. At the time, Moritz also accepted Erich's rendition of the event. Moritz attempted to quiet his sons' resurrected suspicions on this day of Leone's service.

Moritz made an entry in his diary for the sad day of the funeral that "many wreaths and flowers arrived."[3]

Despite the help Erich was receiving with the care of his children and the arrangements for Leone, he seemed to be in a state of both agitation and distress. When he found a moment alone with Moritz, he imposed on him for a loan of $150 for what he said were expenses related to the birth of the newborn and Leone's death. Moritz willingly obliged but the interchange exposed a raw nerve. Moritz would remain silent for now. Years before, when Erich taught at the University of Kansas, Moritz subsidized Erich's inability to support his family. At the time Leone wrote to her sister bluntly, spelling out the news. "Erich cannot afford to pay the board. With best love to you and all, Leone."[4]

Leone's family generously loaned her money, yet the couple fell behind.

> My dear Louise,
> Am so sorry to have delayed sending you at least a part of the money. Leone[5]

It was now three days after the death of his wife and when Erich learned of the cemetery arrangements, he responded that he no longer cared about life and Leone's dust could scatter to the four winds. He refused to be a part of the funeral procession.

Erich left the Krembs home earlier than most of the visitors. He told the family he would visit a friend from the University of Chicago. Leone's parents, her siblings, and the couple's children never laid eyes on him again.

Leone's family made all the necessary arrangements for her body to be cremated at Graceland Cemetery and her ashes buried on Sunday at Rosehill Cemetery.

While the family attended to the funerary details, Erich traveled to 171 La Salle Street, the Chicago office of New York Life Insurance Company. When he arrived at the insurance office, he asked to collect the balance on the policy of $1,000. The life insurance policy for $2,000 was purchased shortly after Erich began tutoring Leone, and she named her mother as beneficiary. A month after the wedding, she changed the beneficiary to Erich. In 1903, a loan of $196 was made to Leone from her policy probably to help subsidize Erich's income or pay back money owed. Then Leone changed the beneficiary, "Erich, in care of Helen." Erich was now the beneficiary of the funds with a moral, but no legal, obligation to provide for the care of Helen.

He produced the necessary papers, a death certificate and burial permit. After waiting, the clerk at New York Life Insurance Company denied his request. Erich protested. The clerk provided Erich with the record entry on November 4, 1905, when the policy was transferred to the New York office. The funds were no longer payable at the Chicago office.

Traveling to New York was not an option for Erich at this time. The money remained in the New York office, but he requested a change of beneficiary from himself to his sister, Mrs. Agnes Münter Gundlack. Agnes spelled the family's surname in its original German lettering with the umlaut.

The Krembs family, sans Erich, were driven to the Rosehill Cemetery, situated along Lake Michigan. That Sunday was gloomy and cold. Their entry into the cemetery seemed to finalize Leone's death. They passed under the Gothic archway adjacent to a bell tower. The structure was built in 1864 and survived the Chicago Fire of 1871.
Moritz wrote in his diary, "The four brothers [were] pall bearers."[6]

Erich, whose location was not known, wrote a letter to his Harvard colleagues. The faculty of the German department admired him. He had a reputation as a first-class scholar, an indefatigable worker, a demanding instructor who gave his students weighty assignments, and a difficult grader. He often spoke quickly and distinctly as a man who had little time to waste. The letter has not survived but the newspapers described it as "incoherent and was evidently written by some person disordered mentally."[7] The letter circulated among the faculty. Albert Morey Sturtevant, a fellow instructor in the German department, read Erich's letter and believed he suffered a mental breakdown due to overstudy and grief. He had visited Erich and Leone at their Oxford Street apartment and described them as a wonderful, loving couple who made him envious of their relationship.

On Tuesday, April 23, Harvard received a letter from Erich announcing his resignation. Then he vanished.

CHAPTER 6

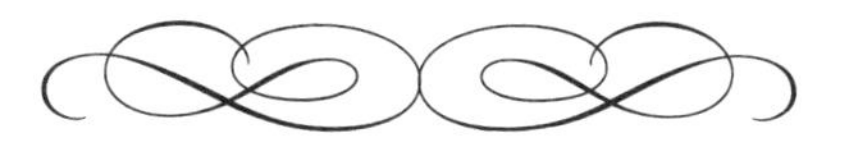

Inheritance Powder

At Massachusetts General Hospital, Dr. Whitney conducted forensic pathological testing on the mucous membrane of Leone's stomach excised at her autopsy. His laboratory was equipped with a "Marsh test" apparatus. According to medical literature in 1896, the "most delicate and accurate method of determining small quantities of arsenic in forensic cases [was] by the Marsh apparatus."[1]

The apparatus was a simple glass tube into which a sample of tissue or body fluid was introduced together with a specific quantity of zinc and acid. If arsenic was present, the solution produced arsine, a poisonous, flammable gas with a garlic-like odor. Leone's sample tested positive.

Whitney also observed an enlarged liver and white particles in the mucous membrane, which, according to *Medical Jurisprudence, Forensic Medicine and Toxicology* by Rudolph Witthaus and Tracy Becker, published in 1894, indicated arsenic poisoning.[2]

Whitney was at the forefront of forensic medicine, but in a courtroom his findings and opinions were not met with universal acclaim. Less than five months before Leone's death, Whitney was called to testify at the inquest in the death of Mrs. Jennie Phillips Chase, a member of the wealthy Phillips family. At the time of her death, Jennie was estranged from her second husband, Dr. Chase. Jennie told friends that

Chase had married her for her money, like her first husband, whom she had divorced.

A week before her death, Jennie told her friend that if she should suddenly die, "something would be wrong" and that her husband was the villain.[3] A servant found Jennie dead on the kitchen floor, along with her canary, parrot, and dog. Her Boston dressmaker and friend testified that she visited the home on the day of Jennie's death, and Dr. Chase told her Jennie died of pneumonia. The medical examiner determined the death to be suicide by gas poisoning. Several days later, after completing forensic testing, Dr. Whitney testified that a large quantity of arsenic, sufficient to cause death, was found in the decedent's throat and stomach. Dr. Whitney was convinced Jennie had been poisoned. The judge presiding at the inquest was not persuaded by Whitney's opinions and findings and found that Jennie had died from "her own acts and the death was one of suicide."[4]

Poisoning was perceived to be the most common form of homicide. Arsenic had gained quite the reputation as a poison of choice, particularly among the wealthy. It was known in nineteenth-century France as the *poudre de succession*. It earned its stature as inheritance powder because it was implicated in 40 percent of murders between 1835 and 1880. Beneficiaries could fast-track bequests with this wondrous substance. It is colorless, odorless, tasteless, and soluble in liquid, a perfect ingredient for surreptitious administration. Small doses of arsenic permanently accumulate in hair, nails, and bone. Children are particularly susceptible. If administered in small doses, it can mimic the symptoms of a progressive natural illness.

Within hours of ingestion, the body reacts with severe stomach pains, causing a person to wrench up and vomit the contents of the stomach. Most of the poison can be eliminated by vomiting or excreting it, causing a reprieve. Repeat doses eventually build up in the lining of the stomach and intestinal tissue. Eventually, the victim may experience bloody vomit and diarrhea, and the skin may become cold and clammy. Sometimes there is a garlic odor and a precipitous drop in blood pressure. The victim may convulse, or the body may begin to shut down and enter a comatose state. When death occurs, it is caused either by dehydration or starvation because arsenic impedes the process of converting food into energy.

On April 27, 1906, twelve days after Leone's death, Whitney issued his report in Leone's case, which confirmed Dr. Swan's suspicions. The report opined that "marked traces of arsenic were found in Leone's organs."[5] Whitney called District Attorney George A. Sanderson, who called the Cambridge police. Electromagnetic pulses buzzed through the telegraph wires to police and newspapers around the country. F. B. Pullen, Cambridge's chief of police, sent the following message with Erich's picture:

> ERICH MUENTER
> WANTED FOR MURDER
> Description: age, about [thirty-five] years; height, about [five foot nine] or [ten] inches; weight, about 150 lbs.; florid complexion, dark hair, long face, slanting forehead, full dark brown Vandyke beard and moustache, good teeth; loose-jointed walker.[6]

The *Evening Herald*'s headline read: "Harvard Teacher Wanted for Murder."[7] The press latched onto the story. Police departments across the country pursued leads on the missing murderer. On April 26, Moritz wrote a note in his diary: "Two detectives called at House inquiring about Erich."[8] The next day, he recorded in his diary, "[Nine] P.M. Reporter said report in Boston that Erich Muenter poisoned his wife. Fifteen to twenty reporters called."[9]

In public Moritz was steadfast in support of his son-in-law's innocence. It likely weighed heavy on his mind that if Muenter was his daughter's murderer, then he played an unwitting role in her death. He had hired Erich to tutor Leone in order to pass a French language exam so she could qualify as a teacher.

When asked by the press about the arsenic, Moritz would not give any credit to this "dreadful story." "My son-in-law is a Christian Scientist. Muenter and my daughter were happy in their married life and there was nothing between them that I know of that would lead him to kill her."[10]

Moritz told reporters that Erich convinced Leone to become a Christian Science member upon marriage. He found Erich to be nervous, highstrung, and opinionated, but absolutely not murderous. He believed Erich considered anyone who disagreed with him "as old fashioned and antiquated."[11]

Moritz repeated the diagnosis Erich articulated: after childbirth Leone developed blood poisoning and because of her Christian Science belief, there had been no medical intervention.

Leone's mother, Johanna, stood by her husband's position and also supported her son-in-law: "My son-in-law is a Christian Scientist and this may have led to the suspicion that my daughter's death was not from natural causes."[12] Where Johanna and Moritz got the idea that Erich was a Christian Scientist is not known.

Eugene, Leone's younger brother, was not so charitable. He broke ranks with the family and spoke out, accusing Erich of the murder. He supported his position with a litany of events: Erich's insistence that the body be cremated, his exculpatory note, his disappearance, his abandonment of his children, and his failure to be forthcoming with the details about his wife's death. With the arsenic report, Muenter's guilt was well beyond speculation or surmise. Eugene conceded that Erich was not in his right mind. He still wanted answers about the last days and hours of his sister's life.

Erich's friend Professor Crowe—the very same man who was present when the gas went out in the apartment years before and whom Erich told of his travel to Chicago with his dead wife—said Erich did not poison his wife. Perhaps he could not be found because he had died by suicide due to the "shock of his wife's death and the blow which followed."[13] Was Crowe speculating or had he been contacted by his friend to derail police from continuing the search?

The front page of the *Boston Daily Globe* featured two pictures, side by side, of Erich Muenter and Leone with Helen sitting on her lap. The headline read: "Muenter Accused of Murder of His Wife, Instructor at Harvard Being Sought by the Police. *Large Quantity of Arsenic Found in the Woman's Stomach.*"[14]

Some newspapers were more cautious about accusing the Harvard instructor and afforded him the benefit of his highly respected reputation.

The Cambridge police and the country's news reporters scurried for any detail or rumor about the missing Harvard instructor and his deceased wife. One reporter titillated his readers with a neighbor's account that "they were so devoted to each other as to arouse joking comments among their friends."[15]

The manhunt and the public fascination intensified.

Pressed by reporters, Dr. Taylor would only admit to the house calls at the Muenter home. He had seen a very sick young woman in need of the most competent medical treatment. McIntire avoided all questions except to say that he had examined Leone.

The press tracked down Bertha Derrick, Erich's neighbor who had accompanied him to Chicago. She was in disbelief about the news. She said she had watched Professor Muenter for hours on the train. She described him as a grief-stricken husband with the deepest affection for his wife and loving fondness for his children.

Finally, the reporters reached the one person who had been at Leone's bedside, Mrs. Edith Chase. "I cannot understand this charge of poisoning, for I do not see how it could be true, judging by what I saw of the man and the way he appeared to think of his wife."[16]

It must have been unthinkable to the woman who was in immediate charge of Leone's care before, during, and after childbirth. The accusation against Erich necessarily implied that the crime happened under her watchful eye.

One reporter chased to find a faculty member at the University of Kansas, where Erich taught after leaving Chicago, who said, "I would as soon think I were guilty of the murder of my own wife as to believe this thing about Mr. Muenter."[17]

Boston's Police Inspector Huxley and District Attorney Sanderson presented the case before Cambridge's District Court Judge Charles Almy. They offered statements of what they believed was the smoking gun—Professor Whitney's report of arsenic poisoning and Erich's disappearance.

Judge Almy listened carefully to the testimony. Six years before he had another high-profile case regarding a professor from his alma mater, Harvard. Almy dismissed the murder charge against Prof. Charles R. Eastman despite the victim's last words incriminating the professor. The public was outraged.

Judge Almy refused to sign a warrant for Muenter's arrest, stating that there was insufficient evidence of murder. The news stories were inaccurate, there was no warrant for Erich Muenter's arrest.

A month went by without a word from Erich. In June, he sent Harvard's President Elliot, his chairman, Prof. Kuno Francke, Prof. Hugo Münsterberg, two faculty colleagues, the Krembs family, and his friend Crowe a strange pamphlet, a disturbing fourteen-page screed titled, "Protest," typed on five-by-seven paper and divided into three sections. Part I was "Sensation! Scandal! Autopsy Cremation Assfixiation [*sic*]."[18] The rant opened with the line "The disgusting details of the next eight pages being nothing but filth and lies, may be admitted with great profit to the reader."[19] The following pages included a bizarre, twisted fictional or pseudo-fictional account of the birth of a child, a professor, Christian Science practitioners, doctors, the death of a wife, an autopsy, a death certificate, two brothers, knives, bullets, gas jets, and a five-gallon can of kerosene.

> "The medical examiner . . . whose naked arm was graded by a bullet, sprang, knife in hand, toward the window . . . So he screamed, 'Don't shoot, Professor Smith. I'll make out the certificate. And I won't say anything about what happened here . . . ' A bullet tore away a portion of his skull, laying open his cunning brain. 'Ah, here is an autopsy for you,' shouted the mad man . . . A five-gallon can of kerosene and a burning match soon made the first pretty flames, lapping their way to the pile further [*sic*] in the room . . . [He] inserted a tube attached to the bathroom gas fixture . . . The murderer then leisurely walked to the room where the nurse was feeding the baby and turned on the two gas jets . . . shut all the doors and windows . . . [and] went out on the front porch."[20]

The recipients of his diatribe had to ask themselves whether he was truly insane or intent on persuading the world he was insane.

CHAPTER 7

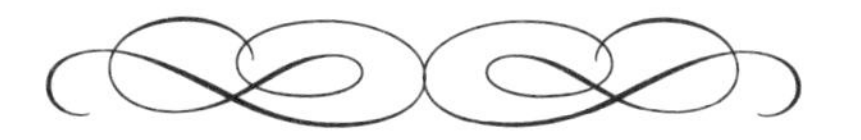

Neared the Truth

Meanwhile, in Cambridge, a Harvard colleague willingly shared with the press his personal experiences with Erich and Leone. He never knew of any friction between them. He claimed it was Erich's preparation for his insanity thesis that worked on his mind and threw him off his mental balance, which might cause him to act irrational but not murderous.

Reporters scampered around to find other acquaintances, however remote. Miss Gahm, a waitress who worked near the Harvard campus, claimed to have befriended Erich. She told reporters how their common German roots bonded them as kindred spirits, and that he had confided in her. She claimed that Erich invited her to dine at his home on a Sunday. When she arrived and knocked on the door, a hostile Leone answered and quite curtly asked her to leave. Leone said that Erich was seriously ill. Miss Gahm told the reporter that there was chatter among other patrons that Erich had such a violent temper and became so angry that it often left him debilitated. Her sensational story could not be confirmed.

But one newspaper, possibly fed the story by an Erich ally, reported that Leone took arsenic for kidney trouble and was addicted to it. Old wives' tales in some parts of the world spoke of arsenic as a means of illuminating a woman's complexion thereby radiating an appearance of youth and good health.

One reporter conjured a possible motive as to why an intellectual at an elite college would murder his wife after childbirth. He was given a letter from an unnamed "friend" of Erich's written before the birth, stating that Mr. Muenter's state of mind is such that if this baby is a girl, his disappointment might cause him to do something rash.

Another reporter wrote that Erich and Leone quarreled when he received letters from a would-be German lover. There was a public thirst for news, and rank speculation would fill the void.

Leone's brother Eugene was again approached by the press and willingly obliged. He called his brother-in-law a murderer. When asked what Erich's motive could possibly be, he simply said it was money. He told reporters that Erich murdered his sister for a $1,000 life insurance policy, the total amount Erich earned yearly. He believed Leone and the two children imposed a financial burden on the Harvard instructor's ambitions. He went on to say that until he appeared and proves his innocence, he was guilty. Eugene did not believe Erich was insane or that he died by suicide.

Leone's brother Walter also weighed in with reporters. He rifled through a coat once worn by Erich and claimed there was white powder in the pocket, which he believed may have contained arsenic. The jacket with the powder was delivered to the Chicago Police Department's central station. Nothing further was heard about the powder.

Leone's mother, Johanna, had no time for reporters. She faced the daily care of three-year-old Helen and a newborn. Helen had been inseparable from her mother and was inconsolable at times. Johanna found it incomprehensible that Erich would permanently disappear and abandon his daughters. She was overwhelmed with the loss of her daughter and the responsibility of her granddaughters. She made her feelings about her son-in-law clear: "Erich Muenter was not worthy of our daughter."[1]

The reporters stalked Leone's sister Louise about the murder accusations. She unleashed her raw private feelings that Erich was not good enough for Leone. She said his focus was not on his family but on mysticism, spiritualism, and strange theories of sex. Louise had an indelible memory of Erich saying, "after reading Oscar Wilde's *Ballad of Reading Gaol,* that each man kills the thing he loves."[2]

It seemed newspaper men were everywhere. One hounded Leone's father Moritz. "His absence and his failure to communicate with us are the strongest evidence against him outside of the presence of arsenic in the stomach as developed by the autopsy."[3] He added, "We did not know until after the funeral that any portion[s] of the body were retained for medical examination."[4]

Chicago newsmen were eager to speak with Erich's colleagues from the University of Chicago. Their investigations turned up evidence of Erich's enigmatic interests. Erich had formed a secret chapter of the Rosicrucian society, whose foundation was a complicated mix of magic and alchemy. A true follower of the Rosicrucian order could see a rising waft of air at the exact moment of a person's death and its psyche or spirit connects with the highest order of Deity. Followers accept that there is no true death but merely a metamorphosis from one physical state to another. The Rosicrucian society was said to believe that their followers had a "high degree of intellectual development."[5]

After Erich's disappearance, his former University of Chicago classmates whom he had not seen in over three years, felt it necessary to hold a meeting at the university's Quadrangle Club. After the meeting, Crowe represented the group's conclusions. He contacted the press and said Erich's disappearance was likely the result of an unbalanced mind due to the tragedy of losing his wife and the mother of his children. They were aligned with Erich's stated explanation—his wife and not he was a Christian Scientist. Her death was a result of blood poisoning and lack of medical care due to her adherence to her beliefs.

Far from Chicago, one energetic reporter on the West Coast was able to get a scoop. He tracked down Erich's mother, Julia, who lived in the sleepy city of Monrovia, near the foothills of the San Gabriel mountains, about twenty-five miles outside of Los Angeles. The reporter waited for Erich's mother to exit services at the Christian Science Church. Then, pen and paper in hand, he accosted her with questions.

Julia, calm and composed, said, "there is no poison but mental poison," and her son was "too tenderhearted"[6] to commit such a crime. She told the reporter that she initially believed that a man who had died by suicide in Philadelphia was her son, but now her feelings on the matter were different. "It is not true—it is not true what they say. My son did not kill his wife. When I received his last letter, I knew how much he loved her. They sent me money but I knew that they were having a hard struggle there. Every letter I received from my son was about such happy lives."[7]

Weeks later, Julia told the *Los Angeles Times* that Leone was brought up a Catholic and had become a "loyal Christian Scientist,"[8] but her son was not. Erich's sister Bertha reiterated her mother's statement. But Leone's family did not agree. Moritz retorted that it was Erich who was a Christian Scientist, and he convinced her to become a Christian Scientist after they were married.

There was additional information that confirmed that Leone was not a Christian Scientist or at least, not for a long period of time. The *Lawrence Daily Journal* reported that when Erich taught at the University of Kansas at Lawrence, Leone was a member of the Unitarian Church.

But Leone's own words tell a different story. In a letter four years before her death to her sister Louise, she indicated her conviction in the core beliefs of Christian Science teachings. "You see medicines fail—leave it to a higher authority . . . all things are possible with God. Hold fast to the thought in 'Science of Being.' . . . I am with much love to you and all the dear ones."[9] The "Science of Being" is a chapter in Christian Science's *Science and Health with Key to the Scriptures,* one of the seventeen published works of Mary Baker Eddy.[10]

Leone wrote an inscrutable note in her letter to her sister in the summer of 1905, that she had "neared the Truth," and as soon as she grew in her understanding of the religion, "I shall not hesitate to join."[11]

The newspapers reported daily that there were speculations as to the whereabouts of the missing Harvard professor. Professor Crowe spoke again to the press. He told the *Chicago Daily News* that perhaps Erich was in a Chicago hospital for treatment of a back ailment. Crowe assured the members of the press that if Erich was alive, he would explain his disappearance and answer their questions.

The circumstantial evidence was mounting against Erich, but there was no physical evidence, no eyewitness, no overheard conversation tying him to arsenic poisoning. To a prosecutor, and perhaps a jury, Erich's sudden disappearance was evidence of guilt. The Middlesex district attorney had too many unanswered questions about the death of the young mother. The autopsy report from Dr. Whitney sat on his desk and could not be ignored. "Arsenic." The evidence pointed to murder by poison.

The district attorney had only one option now, and that was to request an inquest and get answers.

CHAPTER 8

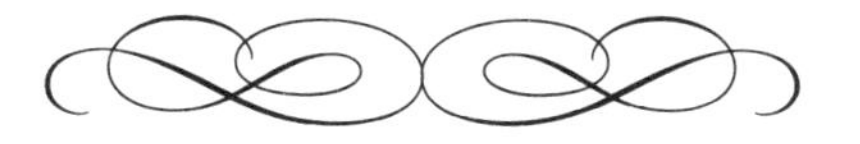

Bertha

Erich's sister Bertha was twenty-four at the time of her sister-in-law's death. Bertha Muenter enjoyed a stellar reputation as a young teacher in Chicago's Hendricks school and lived a carefree life at the Hollenden Hotel, a boarding-style home. Bertha described Erich and Leone as a loving couple who were devoted to each other. She was distraught over Leone's death. Her brother had described the reasons for her death.

Two days before the pathology report was released, Bertha's behavior changed and caught the attention of her friends, colleagues, the police, and the press. Bertha locked herself in her room at the hotel. She took a leave from teaching at school. Her friends and colleagues found her behavior strange, troubling, and uncharacteristic of the Bertha they knew. The press was quick to pick up on Bertha's reclusiveness. One inference drawn was that Erich had made contact with her and she was frightened by the police swarming around her.

Without providing her family, friends, or her school with any information, she made plans to leave for Cambridge, a place she had never visited. Somehow, she figured out how to contact Bryant, the Harvard student who rented a room in the Muenter apartment.

Bertha would not purchase her own train ticket but instead imposed on the hotel proprietor to purchase one for her. The Chicago police received a tip about her departure date and time and waited for her at the station. Bertha thwarted the police and abruptly abandoned her plans to leave on the 10:30 P.M. train on April 27.

On April 28 the newspapers reported that Dr. Whitney found substantial quantities of arsenic in Leone's stomach.

In the early morning hours of April 29, escaping everyone's notice, Bertha boarded a train for Boston.

Her departure may have evaded the Chicago police, but the Boston police were informed of her movements. Two police inspectors were waiting for her at the Muenter apartment. Bryant, Erich's tenant, gave them access.

Bertha rang the bell of her brother's apartment and was met by the police, who informed her that her brother was wanted for the murder of his wife and the apartment was a crime scene. They were there to collect evidence. Bertha became hysterical and left. The police continued to seize items from the couple's home, including a carboy of spring water, milk, jelly, preserves, contents of drinking glasses, and household utensils.

Bertha's bout of hysterics did not last long. She immediately walked to Mrs. Derrick's home, the woman who traveled to Chicago with Erich. Bertha had met Mrs. Derrick only briefly at the Krembses' home. Mrs. Derrick refused to believe the unsubstantiated reports that Erich poisoned his wife.

Bertha had made arrangements while still in Chicago to meet with an attorney, Gilbert A. Pevey, at the Derrick home. Pevey was well connected with Cambridge city government and served as city solicitor. Despite Bertha's lack of legal sophistication and unfamiliarity with Cambridge, she had uncanny judgment—or good advice—in selecting an attorney for her brother. Pevey was well respected and quite capable of representing the Harvard instructor.

After meeting with Bertha, solicitor Pevey left and was met with the press who were waiting for him. "Do you think Muenter is alive?" Pevey answered, "Yes, I do, I have no reason to suspect that he would commit suicide."[1]

Perhaps Erich's sister knew and had told Pevey more than he disclosed to the press. The lawyer said he would refute Dr. Whitney's arsenic findings with a report from another chemist.

Reporters dug up gossip, undoubtedly originating from Leone's brother, Walter, and questioned Pevey. The story dated back to Erich's engagement to Leone. There were scandalous rumors about Erich that stood to ruin Leone and the good name of the Krembs family in Chicago's German community.

Leone and Erich had professed their eternal love for each other and planned to wed. Then suddenly Erich left for Germany, claiming he would study and teach there for a short period. He did not return when he promised he would.

Walter heard that while Erich was in Germany, he had been in an intimate relationship and possibly an undisclosed marriage to a young German woman, and this was the reason why he had delayed his return. Walter contacted relatives and friends in Germany who confirmed the story. Enraged, Walter begged Leone to abandon Erich. Then more news arrived from Germany: the girl jilted Erich when she learned of his engagement to Leone. Erich returned to Chicago as if nothing had happened. Leone would not challenge Erich upon his return.

Pevey dismissed the rumor.

The toughest question Pevey faced was: why did his client disappear if he was utterly innocent? What could he say? His response was along the lines of sometimes those stricken with grief act strangely. It could have been nothing more than that. But it was tough to fight a criminal charge without a client.

With the arrest notice plastered in the papers, Pevey felt the need to tamp down the hype. He sent Bertha Muenter the following telegram with instructions to have the text inserted in paid notices in newspapers: "ERICH MUENTER—It is of the utmost consequence for you to return to Cambridge at once to refute charges made against you. Counsel secured. Do not talk to anyone before you see your sister there. Friends are standing by and will support you."[2] Pevey advised Bertha to make the following statement to the press: "My brother is innocent of any crime. He is not insane and he is not a murderer."[3] She said she would remain in Cambridge until Erich returned.

There was another reason Bertha came to Cambridge. She needed to enter the Muenter apartment. Bryant was eager to collect some of his personal belongings from the apartment. Bertha never disclosed the reason she wanted access to the apartment. Was she looking to remove a hidden item of evidence? From Mrs. Derrick's window, Bertha saw a crowd of reporters waiting for someone to enter or exit the residence at 107 Oxford Street.

Like the reporters, the police had the Muenter and Derrick homes under continued surveillance. There would be no opportunity to leave through the front door. Mrs. Derrick figured out how to circumvent the police reconnaissance. She took Bertha and Bryant to a back staircase. There, behind the homes, was a connecting yard that gave them access to a back door. After nightfall, they crept behind the homes, avoiding the other neighbors. Bryant used his key to open the back door. He went to his room while Bertha rifled through Leone and Erich's personal property, removing certain items. They both returned to Mrs. Derrick's home and slept there overnight.

When the police went to the Derrick home the next day to speak with Bertha, she was gone. Bertha evaded the police but did not evade one determined reporter from the *Detroit Free Press.* He seized the story by securing a seat on Bertha's train from Boston to Chicago. Through a drawn curtain on the lower berth of the Pullman sleeper car at 8:50 P.M., the reporter shouted, "Are you Miss Muenter?" several times.[4] Finally, the curtain was drawn a few inches, "Yes, I'm Miss Muenter; what do you want?" He handed her a telegram from the Cambridge police claiming that she was in possession of evidence of a crime, her brother's diary, and requesting that she submit to police questioning. "There is no truth in it! Not a word! Besides it is not a case of murder, Erich's wife died a natural death." Before she could pull the curtain closed, the reporter told her that the police claimed that she knew "where your brother, Prof. Muenter is at present. Is that true?" Bertha quickly flung the curtain closed while repeating the same answer to a dozen questions, "I have nothing to say."

The Pullman conductor knew nothing of her presence but when questioned by the reporter, he told of Bertha's odd behavior. "She seemed very much in fear of being seen and has eaten nothing all day. I asked her in particular once if she wasn't ill, and if there was anything I could do for her, and she said she wasn't feeling very well, but would be all right." The conductor said that she appeared to read a Bible, but "she seemed not to be reading the printed pages of the Bible as closely as she seemed to be examining some enclosures which it contained, apparently sheets of writing."[5]

The same telegram the reporter on the train delivered to Bertha from the Cambridge police was delivered to the Hollenden Hotel, but it was returned because Bertha no longer resided there. When she returned to Chicago, she went underground and could not be found.

To both the Cambridge and Chicago police, Bertha was a person of interest.

On May 1, a Christian Science doctor, Mrs. John G. Fales, came forward for the first time and told the press that she provided the absent treatment, inaudible prayers delivered from miles away, for Leone in her last days. Leone told her something strange.

When news of Fales's statement broke, the Boston police reentered the apartment. Solicitor Pevey took countermeasures to defend his missing client by requesting that the coroner make Leone's stomach and intestines available for an expert chosen by the defense.

Towing the Pevey line, one headline read "Say Harvard Is Blocking Murder Probe."[6]

Judge Almy again refused to sign a warrant for Muenter's arrest, but after a meeting with Police Inspector Huxley and District Attorney Sanderson, he relented and granted the request for an inquest. It would begin on May 4.

CHAPTER 9

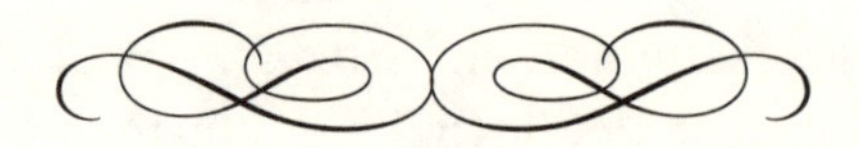

Shock and Surprise

Prompted by the Cambridge "Wanted" notices in newspapers, there were sightings of Erich everywhere: Wayne, Iowa; Omaha, Nebraska; Dover, New Hampshire; Cloverdale, Illinois; Philadelphia, Pennsylvania; and various locations in Germany.

The Cambridge press continued to follow the story and hypothesized that the professor may have poisoned his wife by feeding her arsenic in small doses over a nine-day period. Some in the Harvard community pushed back in reaction to the news and refused to believe a colleague was capable of such a heinous act.

District Attorney Sanderson was swamped with telephone calls and telegraphs responding to the key question that was left out of Dr. Whitney's report. How did the arsenic enter her body? The case presented more questions than answers, although Sanderson had his own theory. If the judge's report of the inquest pointed a finger at a particular accused, a grand jury indictment would follow.

Judge Almy was tasked with writing a report on "where, at what time, by what means, with what instrument and in what manner the party was killed or came by his death."[1] Most importantly, if it could be ascertained, he would give all material circumstances and the name of the person whose criminal act or negligence caused her death. Witnesses could be subpoenaed, such as Edith Chase and the doctors, to answer critical questions under oath. Bertha Muenter escaped and was beyond the court's jurisdictional reach.

Less than one month after Leone died, the inquest was convened at the Third District Court of Cambridge. To protect the reputation of the alleged perpetrator, the judge ordered witnesses testify in his chambers. Also present in the chambers were District Attorney Sanderson, his stenographer, and Captain Hurley from the Cambridge Police. Witnesses would be called to testify one at a time.

Even on this fair day in Cambridge, the red-brick, four-story L-shaped City Building at Elliot Square, with four jutting turrets, black iron spikes over the entrance, a clock tower, and an iron crest, was not a welcoming place. Besides the judge's chambers, the building housed the Cambridge courtroom, twenty-eight jail cells, a firehouse, schoolrooms, a room for public and private meetings, a mechanical room for modern necessities such as a fire alarm and telegraph, and an armory housing unspecified weaponry. It was not easy for first-time visitors to navigate to the judge's chambers.

Judge Almy was unfazed by the tumult caused by the clamoring press outside. The witnesses waited, some more patiently than others, for their turn to testify.

Erich's lawyer, Solicitor Pevey, told the press he had demanded admittance to the proceedings. But Judge Almy sided with Sanderson's objection that the lawyer for the alleged murderer should not be present. There were no further matters to be resolved and the proceedings began.

No transcript of the inquest has survived and, if Judge Almy took notes, he did not include them in his repository papers. But sleuthing reporters waited outside the door of Judge Almy's chambers to converge on each witness as he or she finished testifying. They were not about to be shut out of one of the biggest news stories of 1906. None admitted to eavesdropping or compromising an inside source.

As each witness entered the chambers, Judge Almy instructed the witness that he or she was forbidden to speak with reporters or anyone else about the nature of the questions, their testimony, or any matter related to the inquest. But Judge Almy's orders could not muzzle the press.

The first witness called was Dr. Herbert B. McIntire, a local physician and medical school graduate of the University of the City of New York. Dr. McIntire had been tight-lipped and avoided making detailed statements to the press. Now he would describe his attempts to treat the young woman before and after childbirth. When he arrived at the

Muenter home, he found the situation untenable and illogical. A husband urged the doctor to visit his wife before and after childbirth because she was suffering, yet he accosted him with details about his wife's beliefs in Christian Science and would claim she would reject all treatment.

Why didn't McIntire walk out the door? He simply didn't. Instead, he entered the bedroom where Leone lay with abdominal discomfort. Why didn't Leone tell McIntire to leave? She didn't. Leone described her symptoms. Leone, if she was an adherent of Christian Science, would not believe in or accept *materia medica* or the practice of medical science. McIntire would not be distracted by Leone's husband and stayed focused on his patient.

Erich implored him to return four days after childbirth. On April 10 McIntire returned and found Leone suffering from severe nausea and pain. He was unable to make a diagnosis but there was the possibility she had "summer diarrhea" (also known as "cholera infantum" and the "disease of the season"), although the bacteria usually attacked the intestinal tracts of young children, not adults. The symptoms included violent vomiting, diarrhea, and a high fever. Leone's condition did not quite meet the criteria for a diagnosis of summer diarrhea. When McIntire asked Edith Chase to report on the details of Leone's condition, she refused. McIntire could not attend to the patient, and his prescribed medications and treatment were not given to the patient. He felt unable to perform his duties according to the best medical practices. The doctor made sure the judge understood his reasons for discontinuing his medical services.

Erich would again call McIntire to attend to his wife, but McIntire refused. Dr. McIntire would not allow himself to be the physician who merely observed and monitored the slow, painful death of a young mother. The next time he visited the Muenter home, Leone was dead. Why he did not refuse Muenter's request this time is unknown. Erich wanted him to sign a death certificate and was quite agitated. Dr. McIntire testified how he refused and could not with any level of certainty determine the cause of death. After returning to his office, he called the medical examiner's office.

McIntire was stunned by the report of arsenic poisoning. His treatment was based on prenatal and postnatal condition. He never suspected poisoning and could not answer questions about arsenic.

Next to testify was Dr. Frederick W. Taylor, Harvard Medical School class of 1882. Erich called Dr. Taylor on April 14. When he entered the Muenter home, Erich launched into his spiel about his wife's Christian Science beliefs, but no one asked Dr. Taylor to leave. He examined Leone, who was racked with pain, in extremis, and decompensating. Her condition puzzled Taylor. It was only eight days after the baby's birth, and Leone's pulse was weak, and she had a high fever.

Taylor was not informed of Dr. McIntire's visits. Taylor, known in his circles as a no-nonsense medical physician, cut through the noise of Christian Science and offered what he believed to be life-saving treatment. He was frustrated when Erich grew conflicted between a desire to have his sick wife treated and his commitment to honor her beliefs.

Dr. Taylor wasted no time in recommending radical measures to save her life. He offered medications and the assistance of a nurse. Neither offer was accepted.

When he was called after Leone died, he would not opine on how she died and refused Erich's pleas to complete the death certificate. After leaving, he contacted the medical examiner's office. He was not familiar with symptoms of arsenic poisoning and found it hard to believe that someone would murder the new young mother.

Now Judge Almy wanted to know if Erich had access to arsenic at Harvard. He ordered a Cambridge police inspector to summon Charles Robert Sanger, a professor, chemist, and the director of the technical laboratory of Harvard's medical school, to describe how arsenic might be available to an instructor of philology or other personnel employed by Harvard.

Other Harvard faculty members and colleagues testified, including Dr. Kuno Francke, chairman of the German department, and Frederick E. Bryant, the Muenters' renter.

The *Boston Globe* reported that several of Muenter's Harvard colleagues testified that Muenter was now undoubtedly deranged, and that his mental condition was due to overwork and the shock of his wife's death. They believed that when he recovered sufficiently, he would return and give a convincing account that would show his innocence.

Another witness, undertaker George W. Long, testified he could not oblige the widower's request to transport his wife to the nearby St. Auburn Cemetery without a death certificate or, as Erich assured him, a death certificate he would later receive. He described how disturbed he was to see how Leone's body was on her right side with her knees and arms contracted and stiff, an indication that death occurred more than twenty-four hours before. He testified that her face had a stamp of agony depicting her final moments. Long felt obliged to call the medical examiner's office. When Erich called Long the second time, Long examined the death certificate and prepared the body for travel. Erich told Long he would return to Cambridge after his wife's burial in Chicago. Long initially refused payment, but Erich insisted he pay Long before he boarded the train.

Now Sanderson wanted the judge to hear from the medical examiner. Dr. Swan was unavailable to testify. Dr. Durrell, the Sommerset medical examiner who was part of Swan's autopsy team, testified instead. He described the postmortem visit of the three physicians and Erich's bizarre behavior. When asked about the time Leone died, Dr. Swan's autopsy note reflected that Erich said "she appeared to be sleeping at 10:00 P.M. Apr. 15. He left her alone for the night as did the nurse. He went into her room at 6:00 A.M. Apr. 16 and found her dead. He wished to have the body cremated." It took an hour before the doctors were able to go into Leone's room. Durrell testified that the doctors immediately recognized from the state of the body that the young woman had been dead for some time. Sanderson then asked Durrell to read Dr. Swan's report. "Autopsy showed the peritoneum smooth and glistening. Uterus the size of a large orange. Ovaries and tube normal. Mucous membranes of stomach and parts of intestines impacted and thickened. Liver yellowish. Kidneys show grey streaks . . . and spots of extravascular blood." He concluded with "Analysis of the contents of the stomach and intestines showed presence of arsenic, more than one would expect to find after a medicinal dose."[2] The organ tissue was immediately brought to the pathologist. Dr. Durrell was questioned about the date on the death certificate—April 15. He testified that the rigor mortis state was such that the doctors did not believe Erich's account of the time. The doctors agreed that she died before midnight on Easter Sunday. Dr. Swan would write without the benefit of forensic testing the presenting condition as cause of death, "gastro-duodenitis, following child-birth."[3]

Sanderson now wanted Dr. Whitney, the pathologist, to testify and explain the conditions of the organs and mucosa when delivered to him. Whitney used accepted methods of testing the organs and found marked traces of arsenic. He could not testify as to how and when the poison was ingested.

Judge Almy wanted to hear from the Christian Science providers. Mrs. Dora May Nickerson, "practitioner" and doctor of Christian Science, had been a member of the First Church of Christ since 1892. Students were trained at the Massachusetts Metaphysical College (MMC), founded by Mary Baker Eddy, to become Christian Science practitioners and receive a CSD, or Christian Science doctorate. The college closed in 1889, but doctors of Christian Science were popular in the Cambridge area. She claimed to have received her "doctoral" degree from the MMC, although she remains listed only as a "reader" in their records.

Mrs. Nickerson testified that Leone had hired her months earlier, over Erich's objection. Erich was anxious about the possibility that Leone might become ill while attended by a doctor of Christian Science. He was not an adherent of such beliefs.

According to Nickerson, Leone grew sick three days after the birth. A frightened and concerned Erich telephoned Nickerson at home. Mrs. Nickerson described how she remained in her home and prayed, providing "absent treatment." Without ever visiting Leone, Nickerson diagnosed Leone with an enlarged liver. Nickerson testified that Leone's symptoms subsided.

On the fourth day after the birth, Leone's condition worsened. At around 10 P.M. Erich called Mrs. Nickerson again. She provided another "absent treatment" from her home until one-thirty in the morning. Leone's pain subsided. Erich called Mrs. Nickerson to let her know her long-distance prayers had worked. The next morning, Mrs. Nickerson telephoned Leone to tell her she should take comfort knowing that she was at her bedside, treating her from miles away, from ten at night till two in the morning.

Mrs. Nickerson recalled that, two days later when she learned, perhaps from Edith Chase, that Erich called for the intervention of a medical doctor, she immediately discontinued the absent treatments. Erich's action had violated Christian Science tenets.

A second Christian Scientist practitioner was called to testify. Mrs. Fales testified that Leone told her that the beef tea she'd been served had a strange taste.

District Attorney Sanderson anticipated his questioning of the last and most important witness, the only eyewitness living in the Muenter home and caring for Leone—Edith Chase. He was convinced that he could elicit testimony that would incriminate Erich Muenter.

Sanderson, a tall, muscular, imposing graduate of Yale University and Boston University Law School, held no affection for the Harvard judge. As an assistant district attorney and then district attorney, he was known to be an aggressive prosecutor. He earned this reputation when he was able to reverse a grand jury decision not to indict a wife who shot her husband. He became a household name during the sensational national trial of the murder of Mabel Page. He won the respect of the legal community and the public and years later would serve on Massachusetts's highest court.

Edith described her initial contact with the Muenter family. "I was called in about 10 days before Mrs. Muenter died and found the usual conditions in such cases."[4] She was a neighbor of Erich and Leone, an unsophisticated, matter-of-fact person who was in awe of the Harvard scholar.

When asked to describe the birth, she chronicled the sad story from the beginning. She described the day the baby was born. It was a Friday, and she remembered that the weather was rainy and cool. Everyone seemed to be preoccupied with preparations for the coming Easter Sunday on April 15, shopping for lilies, bonnets, suits, belts, coats, and corsets, all under ten dollars at J. H. Corcoran & Co.

In the early morning hours of April 6, the general sense of anticipation heightened. The expectant mother's face exhibited signs that birth was imminent. At the time of accouchement, Edith and Erich were by Leone's bedside. Within minutes, the baby was born and placed in her mother's loving arms. She described Erich as elated that all had gone well. Leone glowed. Within hours, Leone was beginning to regain her strength and was her bright, energetic, cheerful self. She cuddled and fed the newborn. Leone introduced the new member of the family to her sister, three-year-old Helen. Edith noted that the young mother's anxiety subsided as she realized her baby was healthy. The newborn slept in a crib next to Edith's cot beside Leone.

Leone was cautious and followed the customary postpartum instructions of resting and consuming nourishing foods. Edith was conscientious in her care of Leone. She prepared beef tea using the traditional recipe of boiling meat on the bone with an onion or garlic, then simmering it in water for an entire day, creating a slightly viscous elixir as recommended in the book *Notes on Nursing* by Florence Nightingale. "Beef tea may be chosen as an illustration of great nutrient power in sickness."[5] It was said to cure all that ailed you, including lack of energy or sleep, sallow, loose skin, weak joints, or a depressed immune system.

Sanderson inquired whether only Edith brought food to Leone. She was not; her loving husband also cared for Leone.

Edith testified that, the day after the birth, all were healthy. The entire household was serene, with only happy sounds of the crying and cooing of a newborn and the childish voice of Helen. Leone was in excellent health. She was enchanted with her new baby girl and anxious to write a long letter to her family back in Chicago and let them know that all was well.

On Monday, three days after the baby was born, Leone started to experience abdominal pain. Edith speculated that Leone's stomach problems were from food. Perhaps her stomach was compromised due to childbirth. Edith tried to comfort her by giving her milk. Then the wave of sickness ended, and Leone rested. She held and fed her newborn.

In the early evening hours after supper, Leone's stomach started to burn as if someone had lit a fire inside of her. It was so painful she was unable to hold the newborn. In the following days, Leone vomited and the contents contained some blood. Edith was convinced it was something she ate. Erich told Edith he was frightened. He called the Christian Science Dr. Nickerson, and her "absent treatment" seemed to work. And then the sickness returned, with the insufferable burning sensation in her abdomen, the violent retching, and the diarrhea. Edith and Erich alternated at Leone's bedside, day and night, desperately trying to build her strength by giving her sips of liquid that she could hardly retain.

According to Edith, Leone's physical pain became excruciating, and her emotional pain, caused by the separation from her daughter and newborn, was agonizing. She was deprived of any peace.

Edith went on to describe how on Thursday and Friday, Leone was wrenching up more blood than ever before. There was blood in her urine, and she was experiencing muscle cramping and quivering. Mrs. Nickerson was called again on Thursday and continued her "absent" treatments. Erich was distressed and broke with the Christian Science treatment by calling medical doctors. Edith corroborated Mrs. Nickerson's testimony that she discontinued treatments when she became aware of the call to medical doctors. Edith heard Erich call another Christian Science practitioner, Mrs. Mary Fales. "Mr. Muenter assured her that no more physicians would be called in."[6]

Leone's pain came in waves—vomiting, diarrhea, and then calm. The stomach pain would cause her to double over in pain. The interval between symptoms became shorter, leaving less time for any reprieve.

Eight days after the baby's birth, Leone became restive and was unable to find comfort, only gnawing pangs of pain.

Edith remembered Erich calling Dr. Taylor on April 14 and telling the doctor, "I wish you would come over and tell me how sick my wife is."[7]

The atmosphere in the small apartment had become increasingly tense.

As Edith remembered it, "with the permission of her husband I went out for a walk. When I came back she seemed better. Then I was told that the physician, Dr. Taylor whom I had passed as I went out, had given her some nourishment."[8]

She never knew of any prescribed medications. Her duty was to stay at Leone's bedside. Before she left on Easter afternoon, she looked in on Leone. Her body was still, and her eyes were closed. She was no longer wrenching or moaning. To Edith, she seemed peaceful. Edith thought that perhaps the worst of her illness was over.

Easter evening, for the first time Edith did not sleep at Leone's bedside.

"I was in the room all the time with Mrs. Muenter and the baby. The baby was in the crib, and I slept on the cot. About midnight, Mr. Muenter told me I had better go to bed and he would watch his wife during the night. I said I did not feel tired, but he said I should get some rest."[9]

Edith moved her cot and the infant's crib into the nearby dining room. Edith believed Erich remained at Leone's bedside. Edith described how Erich came to her room in the morning and told her he stayed with Leone all night, fell asleep around 4 A.M., and when he woke at 6 A.M., she was dead.

Sanderson was satisfied that he met his burden by eliciting from Edith a vivid description of the suspicious activity by the only other person in the apartment—Erich. He had no further questions, but the reporters had many.

"Had you at any time any suspicion that the young woman was being given poison?"[10]

"Why, of course I did not."

"What opportunity did Mr. Muenter have to give his wife food or drink without your knowledge?"

"Why, I suppose he had a good many."

"How was he the morning he told you?"

"Why, he acted rather nervous and grief-stricken, but I thought he was very much affected by his wife's death."

"Did he seem to be anxious to hurry the preparations for the disposition of the body?"

"Yes, but it was because he was anxious to start as soon as possible for Chicago with the body."[11] Edith would not allow anyone to plant seeds of doubt in her mind.

"There is nothing I can say about Mr. Muenter except that he seemed anxious to do what he could for his wife. When she had the trouble, he was worried and wanted to call doctors. During all the time I was there, there was nothing that I saw which now makes me think that Mr. Muenter acted strangely."[12]

The inquest was over. On the judge's desk was Leone's death certificate with the cause of death, "gastro-duodenitis, following child-birth," and the pathologist's report, "arsenic."[13]

After three days of hearing testimony, reporters anxiously waited for Judge Almy's report. No report was ever released to the public, no warrants were issued, and no finding of an intentional homicide was made.

Neither Sanderson nor Almy ever knew of the entry Leone's father, Moritz, made in his diary on May 11, 1906: "Examined child & came to conclusion that spots came from arsenic. Small . . . spots, some with pimples, skin hard, peeling off. Stools soft freely, greenish yellow, offensive smell. Ordered physician."[14]

The next day's entry read "Physician Troudy called noon & said symptoms corresponding with arsenic poisoning."[15]

Moritz's diary entries about the newborn would not come to light for more than one hundred years.

CHAPTER 10

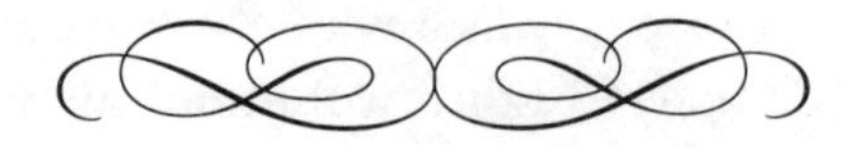

Polytechnic

A clean-shaven Frank Holt easily melded into the fabric of Mexico City. It was an attractive destination for Germans in 1906. Germans had worked the rich mining deposits since 1536. By the end of the nineteenth century, German neighborhoods had their own doctors, teachers, and pastors. One paper, *Mexico Nuevo,* reported, "the German colony in our country we can state without exaggeration that it is one of the most respected in our land."[1] The arrival of yet another single man of German heritage would hardly be noticed.

Frank's command of languages—German, English, Spanish, and French—gave him easy opportunities to work as a stenographer. Stenographers were required to have many skills, including bookkeeping, speed and accuracy in taking dictation, and typing. The newspaper advertisements listed the required skills such as "rapid, accurate, neat, trustworthy, strictly businesslike."[2] Multiple language skills gave job applicants more opportunities. The average salary was nine dollars a week. Samuel Hermanos & Co. of Mexico City, a successful government contractor, found Frank's skills above average and hired him. Within three months, he left Hermanos and started working for Krupp, the German munitions maker. Mexican president Porfirio Díaz was courting the German company Krupp and distancing himself from American businesses.

At the Chicago Columbian Exposition thirteen years before, the Krupp Pavilion exhibited the world's largest cannon known as "Big Bertha," in honor of Bertha Krupp. By 1906, Krupp was engaged in design and construction of the first U-boats. The U-boats were central to Germany's plan to wrest naval superiority from Britain.

All did not go as smoothly as Frank had hoped. Residing in the same boardinghouse was a professor of modern languages from Texas A&M who wanted to learn Spanish. The American professor was intrigued with Frank's language proficiency. Frank tried to keep his distance, but he felt it wasn't going well. He became paranoid and purchased a revolver. Then he told his employer that he had to quit because of dizziness and fatigue due to the high altitude, 7,350 feet above sea level.

Frank traveled to the small city of El Oro de Hidalgo, about one hundred miles northwest of Mexico City and found work as a stenographer for Oro Mining and Railway Company. Another American was working there, James Dean. Frank would not engage in small talk with Dean or anyone else. But his guarded demeanor and penchant for privacy only stoked curiosity.

After nearly a year in Mexico, Frank was again on the move. He assessed the situation and crossed into the United States at San Benito, Texas. San Benito was an arid tumbleweed wasteland due to its resacas, meandering former channels of the Rio Grande, which were either dry or contained stagnant ponds and marshes. The San Benito Land and Water Company hired Frank as a stenographer. The company began constructing canals to connect the resacas with a pumping station on the Rio Grande, at Los Indios, allowing the fresh water to flow through San Benito. It advertised the land in the *Brownsville Daily Herald* as "The most favored spot, in this the most favored valley on the continent."[3]

It was impossible, at least in Frank's mind, for a man of his intellect and ambition to continue as a mere stenographer. He was thirty-six years old. He set his sights on Fort Worth, a cattle town with a population of 27,000. Its inhabitants included demoralized veterans of the Confederate Army who had fought to protect the institution of slavery, which had enabled white settlers to have their fertile, rich land plowed and planted with corn, wheat, and cotton. The townspeople had developed a reputation for hard drinking, gambling, and carousing. Frank was no stranger to the area. He had been there before.

After considering his options, he focused on a small southern institution called Polytechnic College, a Methodist school that had opened its doors in 1891. The college placed advertisements in the local newspapers: “A college with standard curriculum, a first-class preparatory school maintained, a college of fine arts unsurpassed in the Southwest, thirty new pianos ordered.”[4]

The president of the college’s Board of Trustees was a Methodist preacher, Rev. Oscar Fitzgerald Sensabaugh. His daughter, Leona, was one of only four female students at the college and had been accepted directly out of high school. Her father’s position on the board enabled her to attend tuition-free. Leona was neither shy nor a beauty.

Bible classes and attendance at religious services were mandatory for all students. Male and female students were prohibited from interaction, except in very limited circumstances, such as church services. The school circulated a notice, “We are out of the City and our Students are not allowed to visit it except by special permission. We have no gambling halls, whiskey saloons, or other dangerous places to lure young men from virtue’s path.”[5]

Leona embraced college life with gusto. She played tennis and was a member of the volunteer band, a member of a literary society, secretary of the freshman class, a member of the editorial staff of the *Polytechnian,* and vice president of her junior class. She was in line to become president of the senior class. The 1908 yearbook endeavored to capture her essence with the quip, “Suffice it to say, she makes records in subjects in which other young ladies are noted merely for their failure.”[6]

Leona was always available to assist her father with services at the Southern branch of Methodist Episcopal Church.

Frank Holt enrolled as a student at Polytechnic in January 1908. He told his classmates he had purchased a ranch on the Texas side of the Rio Grande and was en route to Chicago when he decided to stop off at Fort Worth. He described how he took the trolley and alighted at the college, where he met with the deans. They were captivated by his linguistic abilities and invited him to attend the school. It was said that he was able to recite Horace’s *The Odes* in Latin with a Southern drawl.

After James F. Sigler, professor of English literature, told the young college men about the arriving new student, they stood and watched as the horse pulling Frank’s carriage ran away after kicking Frank in the shin and leaving him with a nasty bruise. Frank would not succumb to the pain and be embarrassed.

The faculty and students of Polytech were unaccustomed to students with the abilities and credentials of Frank Holt. He claimed he received schooling in Paris, Berlin, and Brussels, and had demonstrated a superior command of languages. He would say that his language skills initially came from his parents, who were born in the United States but were of German and French descent. The faculty recognized his advanced skills and reported foreign education, which allowed him to register as an upper classman—the same class as Leona.

When a full-time faculty member died during the semester, the chairman of the German department tapped Frank as substitute instructor. As a student, he was described as indefatigable, but as an instructor, he was not popular. He demanded excellence from his students. He socialized with other students but only those he felt were of superior intellect.

Frank plunged into school activities. He was designated class poet and accepted as a member of the Philosophian Society, which was dedicated to "attaining that breadth of mind and soul which marks the true scholar."[7] He set his sights on running for the position of vice president of the senior class and was victorious. This strategically placed him second in command to Leona, who was elected class president. By necessity, an exception was made to Polytechnic's strict policy against female students interacting with male students. Leona could not escape the charms of the mature and handsome Frank Holt.

He was fully up to date on national and international news and could dominate discussions on a wide array of scholarly topics that went beyond the focus of his studies. Frank's knowledge of world events and fierce intellect intrigued many in Fort Worth, and his pronounced Texas drawl made him an accessible figure. He seemed worldly and fascinating yet believed in the same humanitarian causes as many others. He tried his best to hide bouts of chronic back pain, for which he had previously had surgery. This malady was the cause of his distinctive disjointed walk.

He faithfully attended the services officiated by the presiding elder, Reverend Sensabaugh, at the local Methodist Episcopal Church, South.

At church and in school, it was impossible for Leona not to become intrigued by Frank.

CHAPTER 11

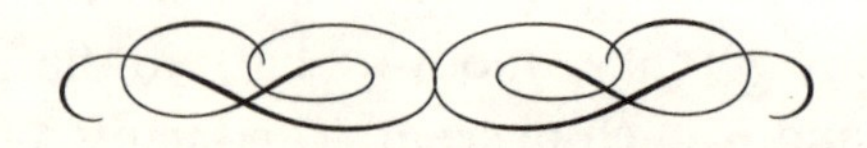

May Be Wooed

Eventually, Frank would confide in Leona about his past. He revealed he was born in Wisconsin, and sadly, both his parents were dead. He had no siblings. He was educated in Chicago as well as schools in Europe. He won her trust and friendship. He sent her a poem he had written years before, or so he said, "of a man, who sought to do good, who did great good, and whose life was shattered by unjust criticism from men who raised him over his grave."[1]

Leona had always been surrounded by a large, loving family, four brothers, a sister, her father and stepmother. The Sensabaugh world centered around Leona's father, who instilled in his children an affection for spirituality, hard work, and honor. Reverend Sensabaugh wrote a memoir documenting his religious journey, which made only a fleeting reference to Leona's mother, who died before Leona's second birthday. Two years after her death, he married Daisy Lane and had two more children.

In his memoir, Reverend Sensabaugh mentioned Leona as a baby. "On Sunday morning, I would roll the buggy in front of the pulpit where she would lie and much of the time watch her father preach. As I remember, seldom did she in any way disturb the service."[2]

In 1909, Polytechnic College published its yearbook, the *Panther City Parrot.* In the first pages of the yearbook, there is a profile photo of the president, "Miss Sensabaugh," and on the very next page is a picture of the vice president, "Mr. Holt," sporting eyeglasses. Frank chose for the quotation under his photo a part of a 133 stanza of Lord Byron's *Don Juan:*

> Man's a strange animal and makes strange use;
> Of his own nature and the various arts;
> And likes particularly to produce;
> Some new experiments to show his parts.[3]

Under Leona's photo, she chose a quote from Shakespeare's violent, bloody, and obscure play, *Titus Andronicus:* "She is a woman, therefore may be wooed: / She is a woman, therefore may be won."[4]

After graduation, Leona went her separate way to work for a year in Cuba. The island still bore scars from Spanish soldiers who brutalized Cubans in the 1898 Spanish-American War. Frank would wait for her return.

The position of chairman of the language department at Polytechnic became available and Frank lost no time in applying. His reputation for academic excellence was beyond challenge, and Leona's father, who was fond of him, was still president of the college's Board of Trustees. Dr. Hiram Abiff Boaz, the college president, recognized Frank as having exceptional studious habits. Frank had every reason to believe he would be confirmed by the board.

But there was a hitch. As part of his application, Frank needed to supply a letter of reference from a recognized scholar attesting to his excellence in the field. He reached out to Texas A&M Prof. Charles B. Campbell, the man who boarded with him in Mexico and whom he had ignored. Though he happened to be a language professor, Campbell's letter was vague.

The reverend's fellow board members and faculty endeavored to do their due diligence. The board recognized the reverend's preference for the young scholar and pursuer of his daughter. But they refused to accept Frank's inadequate, undocumented academic background. To the shock of Reverend Sensabaugh and his protégé, Frank Holt, his application for a faculty position was rejected. His abilities and talents were stellar. His hazy past was the problem. As a student applying for admission, it was unnecessary for Frank to provide documentation of his studies in European institutions. But the faculty chairmanship was held to a different standard. The board found the lack of academic records to be fatal.

And there was also a question about his conduct. It was reported to the board that a revolver had been found in Frank's room. Firearms were strictly forbidden under college rules. Students and faculty were aware of the penalties for such a transgression. The board gave Frank an opportunity to address this revelation, but Frank's explanations were weak and unsatisfactory. He claimed he never carried the gun, but he bought it while he was in Mexico and forgot that it was at the bottom of his trunk. He said he disposed of the revolver immediately when he realized it was still in the trunk. Years later, the board's true opinion of Frank was revealed by board member W. T. Andrews, who said he did not vote for him along with the majority of the board because his past was undocumented. Frank could not satisfactorily answer any questions about his life prior to 1908.

Frank was embittered, but he soldiered on. When Leona returned from Cuba, Frank pursued her with passion and fervor. Within a month of her return in 1910, Reverend Sensabaugh blessed the union and officiated at the wedding. The newlyweds would leave the family and Fort Worth area so that Frank could pursue teaching opportunities at other universities.

For the 1910–11 school year, Frank secured an adjunct faculty position at the University of Oklahoma in Norman, about 185 miles north from the Sensabaugh home. Leona tended to her spousal duties and supported her husband's ambitions at the university. Despite her college degree, she did not work outside the home, which might reflect poorly on Frank.

Frank's contract was not renewed at the University of Oklahoma after charges had been made that he secured his position through church connections. The University Board of Regents included a minister and two church members.

The next stop was six hundred miles east, Vanderbilt University in Nashville, an institution originally connected with the Methodist Episcopal Church. Frank's contract was for one year teaching French. Here he morphed from socialite to recluse, who rarely communicated with other faculty members and refused to allow the university to take his picture. His one-year contract at Vanderbilt was not renewed.

The couple's next move was up the coast, three hundred miles to Emory, Virginia. Frank was hired as an adjunct professor of French at Emory and Henry College. The college listed Frank with an A. B. Polytechnic College and that he was a "Graduate Student, Cornell University."[5]

Leona, who had been so active in school prior to her marriage, now had a passive role as wife in a location far from home. By August 1912, she was pregnant. This gave her life a new purpose. In the spring of 1913, Leona and Frank welcomed their first child, a baby boy, and Frank was easily persuaded to name him after Leona's father, Oscar. Leona had the baby at home without the assistance of a physician because Frank expressed a hatred for all medical men. He immediately secured two $1,000 life insurance policies on himself and a twenty-year-endowment policy for his wife in the sum of $5,000 with Traveler's Accident Insurance Company of New Jersey through a local agent in Tennessee.

The 1913 school year ended and so did his teaching stint at Emory and Henry College. Before the close of the semester, Frank wrote to Andrew Carnegie, the steel magnate, whose philanthropy helped the people of China, asking him for a position as a teacher in China, and for his wife as a missionary. He requested a total salary of $1,500 a year. The application was denied. Without skipping a beat, he shifted his focus to the Ivy League school he listed on his Emory and Henry College application, Cornell University. He applied to Cornell's doctoral program and began his studies in September 1913.

Frank, Leona, and young Oscar traveled to Ithaca, New York, where the weather can be unwelcoming for those raised in a humid, southern climate. Ithaca's winter months can be gray, long, and hard. Sleet and snow can fall from November through April. For Leona, Ithaca could just as well have been Nome, Alaska. It was only three years before that Leona was in the warmth of her family home in Amarillo, Texas. Now, this granddaughter of a Confederate surgeon felt the chill of the "North."

Frank's application to Cornell detailed his studies at European universities and the year of graduation from a small, little-known college in Fort Worth at the age of thirty-five. It is unknown whether Frank disclosed his rejection for a faculty position by the Polytechnic Board, or his past as an itinerant academic at three other institutions. There is no evidence that the Cornell faculty ever questioned his curriculum vitae. Unlike other faculty members listed in *The Cornellian,* the yearbook, Frank is listed with a degree from Polytechnic but without the year of graduation.

Frank was elated to be accepted into the PhD program. He had reached a place worthy of his abilities. Cornell was a premier institution that counted William Strunk among its faculty and could rival, according to some, the reputation of Harvard. Frank was offered a position as an instructor of elementary German. The pay was not intended to be a faculty salary but rather a stipend for graduate students, The standard tuition was $125 per semester. The average grade-school teacher's salary in New York was $975 per year. A full professor at Cornell in 1908 earned $3,143 per year. Frank's salary would be $1,000 a year. He would earn extra money tutoring and teaching in the summer session as he had done elsewhere. He contacted a local tutoring service provided by Comy Sturgis. Sturgis paid him $500 a year to tutor students in foreign languages. Comy found Frank to be a good tutor with an excellent knowledge of the subjects, although he described him at times as discouraged or depressed. Supporting a family on Frank's salary was a struggle.

He became fully engaged with the faculty and was an active member in the Cornell German Club. He made time to attend the meetings of the Philological Club. He kept abreast of both local and international news reading the local newspaper, the *Ithaca Journal.*

At home, Frank was withdrawn, and his views became more liberal, but Leona would later say that he absolutely was not a socialist. She found him kind and caring and, at times, displayed courage. On a ride through the backroads of Ithaca, Frank became incensed watching a man mistreat his horse. Leona beamed with pride when her husband confronted the man without hesitation despite Frank's lean physique.

Frank made time to explore his longtime fascination with mysticism. Cornell's library boasts the most complete collection of works on mysticism. Frank's days and nights were consumed with teaching, tutoring, writing a thesis, and his responsibilities as a father and husband.

Scholarship in the field of philology was recognized as rigorous and scientific. Philologists' research was of such a specialized nature that usually the only attendees at a lecture were other philologists. Frank would sprinkle into his discussions allusions and witchcraft in Shakespeare's *Macbeth* and Goethe's popular novel *Die Leiden des jungen Werthers,* or *The Sorrows of Young Werther.* Goethe told the story of unrequited love about an obsessive-compulsive genius and his infatuation with a young woman. Eventually, young Werther's passion would drive him to suicide.

The Holts settled into a cottage that they leased from a local lawyer, Thomas J. Reidy. Within months, they moved into an apartment at 121 Maple Avenue, a five-minute walk to the Cornell campus.

Along with his academic responsibilities, Frank micromanaged the couple's life. Leona was quite capable of budgeting household expenses, but Frank would not cede control. She was granted an allowance calculated to the exact penny and excluded from information about the household finances.

Frank's taciturn behavior at home did not diminish his appetite for sex. Eight months after Oscar was born, Leona was pregnant again.

Part II

J. P. Morgan Jr.

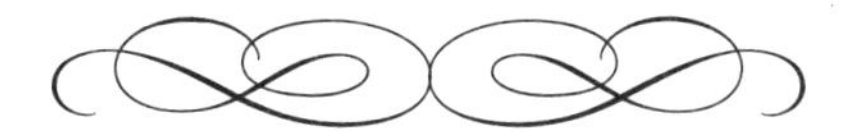

It were better for the most of People to be poor than to be born rich. For such have, in general, really a more comfortable Life here and far less dangerous as to the next Life. . . . A Rich man has a *miserable* life: for he is always full of Fear and Care. . . . Whereas a man that has but food and raiment with honest labour, is free from these fears and cares . . . We need to *pity* and *love* Rich Men.

REV. JOSEPH MORGAN, 1732 SERMON

CHAPTER 12

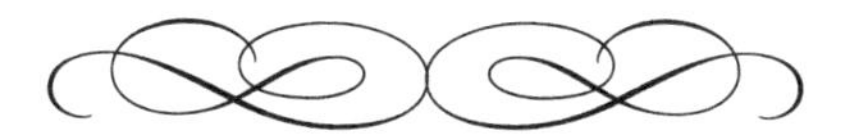

J. P. Morgan

Jack and Jessie Morgan were chatting with the English ambassador and his wife on the Fourth of July weekend at their Long Island estate, Matinicock,[1] while they waited for their guests to arrive. The Morgan mansion was well suited to entertain the aristocratic elite with forty-one rooms, fourteen-foot ceilings, sixteen baths, eighteen massive marble fireplaces, twelve guest rooms and seven children's rooms. There was a private telephone, an enunciator system for communication between family and staff, and an electric elevator.

The newlyweds would arrive in the afternoon. This morning the Morgans were very much at ease with Sir Cecil and his wife. Jack and Jessie were Anglophiles. As a child and young adult, Jack visited his grandfather, Junius, many times in London. Junius lived in a five-story townhouse facing Hyde Park, and he had a twenty-bedroom country home on ninety-two acres on the Thames River. Junius acquired his fortune as a banker at Peabody & Co. in London. The firm evolved into J. S. Morgan & Company, a transatlantic bank.

As a young married couple in 1908, Jack, Jessie, and their three children were sent by Jack's father, Pierpont, to London, to work at his late grandfather's bank. Pierpont's directive to his son was to learn the English central bank system, anchored by the Bank of England, and add new partners to a new partnership agreement. Eventually, the London firm was renamed Morgan Grenfell. Jack's assignment seemed somewhat strange to the London banking partners since Jack, the presumptive heir of the House of Morgan, did not control the banking operations in the London firm. Pierpont made him a partner in Morgan locations in New York, Paris, and Philadelphia, but not London.

Jack's responsibilities in the London office were so minimal that in a letter to his mother, he said that the London office "is where the profoundest peace reigns."[2]

Pierpont gave no indication to Jack of when he would be permitted to return to work in the New York firm Morgan & Co. The young family needed suitable living arrangements near London. Jack's grandparents' home might have served as a fine temporary residence, but Jack was more than comfortable financially and leased a townhouse at No. 2 South Street, at the corner of Park Lane, London. In January 1901, Jack had a front-row seat at the windows of his townhouse across from Hyde Park to watch the funeral procession of Queen Victoria. "Everyone has gone into mourning; you never saw anything so black as the streets."[3] And he witnessed the proclamation of Edward VII as monarch in front of St. James Palace, which was "exactly like a scene in one of Shakespeare's historical plays."[4] President Theodore Roosevelt appointed Jack as a member of the American delegation to the coronation.

Life was good in London. No expense was spared for Jack, Jessie, and the children. There were butlers, nannies, footmen, cooks, and tutors. Their children adopted a "Victorian avoidance of feeling of expression."[5] Jessie often read to her children classic works, such as the *Pickwick Papers* and *The Water Babies,* omitting parts the children would not understand or that she felt were offensive. Jack spent time grouse hunting, and he and Jessie attended theater and dinner parties.

They lived life at the top rung of the social ladder. Pierpont orchestrated social engagements for the young couple, such as the presentation of Jessie to Queen Victoria, and a special invitation for Jack to attend the Levee held by the Prince of Wales. Jack wrote to his mother, "Everyone treats us as if the Morgan family owned the earth, which makes it very pleasant for us."[6] Perhaps they didn't own the earth, but Pierpont and Junius had bought or sold a decent slice of it.

Jack and Jessie were guests at an endless array of dinner parties that included notables such as Mark Twain, Rudyard Kipling (Jack was not overly impressed), the King of Sweden, and Sir Colin Scott, engineer of Egypt's irrigation of the Nile River Basin.

Jack was spending more time with his family and less time on the family business. It was no secret to anyone that Pierpont, Jack's father, was the force behind the House of Morgan. One author ascribed the success of the firm to "the personal quality of [Pierpont]."[7]

Without further direction from his father as to his return to New York, in the spring of 1901, Jack rented a country home, a castle in Hertfordshire, England. It was a mix of the stately but with modern conveniences, featuring four-turrets and central heating. The castle, called, Aldenham Abbey, was six thousand square feet on three hundred acres and included a farm and a lake. To enhance his weekend enjoyment, Jack purchased his first automobile. On Fridays, he would motor the eighteen miles from the London office to Aldenham.

He quickly took to country life and wrote his mother "The farm is most entertaining, and I expect soon to appear in the office with leather gaiters and a straw in my mouth instead of a cigar."[8]

Years later, Jack would offer his home to Ambassador Joseph P. Kennedy Sr. and his family as a refuge from the London blitz during the Second World War. Kennedy graciously accepted, but his stay was short-lived. His views on the war were out of step with Franklin Roosevelt's and he was recalled to Washington.

Jessie was equally enchanted and loved gardening. A farmer provided the family with fresh milk daily. Jack hunted on the estate. The family attended Sunday services at St. John's in nearby Watford, a 750-year-old gothic church adorned with an eleventh-century Norman stained-glass window. After nine years, Jack purchased the Aldenham estate in his wife's name and restored it to its former name, Wall Hall.

While in London, Jessie gave birth to their fourth child, Henry Sturgis Morgan, named after Jessie's father, Henry Sturgis Grew. Jack looked at the newborn and saw a resemblance to his own father, "The ears and setting of the eyes are exactly like—let us hope he may help as many people during his life."[9]

The affection Jack seemed to have for his father did not appear to be returned. Pierpont likely saw Jack as lacking in guts and guile in the aggressive, unforgiving banking world. Pierpont promulgated a firm rule that seemed to intentionally exclude Jack from participating in the New York firm's decision. If a partner was out of the New York office for more than two consecutive weeks, he lost the right to vote or speak for the firm. There was a carve-out for Pierpont, of course, who had extensive trips abroad.

Jack did harbor a mild disquietude when his father insisted on micromanaging transactions remotely from abroad, often through telegrams. "It makes work a little complicated to have [father] out of the office when he wished to decide many questions himself."[10] But if Jack was bothered by his exclusion from the power center of the Morgan business, he never really complained.

While Jack was playing the role of a British aristocrat, his father was orchestrating a merger to create and finance the largest steel operation in the world, US Steel. Within three months, the *New York Tribune*'s front-page headline was "Steel Terms Outlined. Morgan Circular Shows That Capital Stock Will Be $850,000,000."[11] Pierpont did not flinch when he committed half a billion for Carnegie Steel. He also combined competing railroad lines to form Northern Securities.

While Jack was in London, his father excluded him from negotiations of a massive loan to the British Treasury to fund the Second Boer War. Jack had to feel slighted and demoralized by his father's actions.

CHAPTER 13

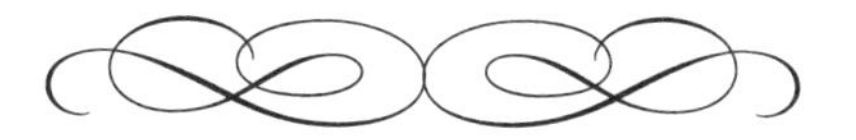

Your Loving Son, Jack

Jack remained loyal to his father his entire life. Pierpont's temperament was gruff and impatient. Jack was quiet and caring. But the physical resemblance between the two was uncanny. Photos of each at different phases of life require more than a glance to determine identity. Jack's physique, at over six feet tall, and his facial features were almost identical to Pierpont, but he was spared his father's bulbous nose, which made Pierpont self-conscious and camera-shy his entire life. There is little evidence of a warm, affectionate father-son relationship. Both Jack and his mother seemed emotionally isolated from his father.

Pierpont found his wife's strong attachment to Jack to be appalling: "His Ma! is scarcely willing to have him out of her sight." "I have abandoned years ago all attempts to separate mother and boy."[1]

In 1871, Pierpont purchased a summer home for the family on a 368-acre estate, in Cragston-Highland Falls, New York, adjacent to the United States Military Academy at West Point. Jack at an early age was able to enjoy the lakes and streams, the horses, and all that country life had to offer.

The center of Pierpont's universe was the island of Manhattan, 23 Wall Street, dubbed The Corner, a six-story office building. Pierpont purchased a brownstone home at 219 Madison Avenue for $225,000 (approximately $6.7 million today) from John Jay Phelps, a railroad baron and financier in 1881. Pierpont's home was one of the first to be illuminated with electric lights, a fringe benefit of being an early investor in the endeavors of Thomas Edison. In a rare father-son outing, Pierpont took Jack on a visit to Edison's laboratory in Menlo Park. In later years, Pierpont arranged the merger of Edison General Electric Company and Thomson-Houston Electric Company, creating General Electric.

Until the age of thirteen Jack had been tutored at home. When the time came for Jack to be launched, his father sent him 250 miles from home to St. Paul's School, in Concord, New Hampshire, the prep school favored by the Vanderbilts and Astors, perhaps an attempt to loosen the mother-son bond. The surroundings were idyllic with wooded trails and beautiful ponds, but Jack found it to be a harsh existence. Rector Coit, the school's headmaster, summed up the place: "This school is an absolute monarchy, of which I am the head, and you must obey my rules or get out."[2] The rigorous curriculum of math, history, science, Greek, and Latin was stressful for Jack, even though he always ranked in the top third of his class. He wrote to his sister Louisa: "How nice it must be to be a girl and be educated at home."[3]

Mother and son committed to exchange letters twice a week while he was at school. His salutation was always "Dearest Momma" and signed "your loving son Jack."

Jack attempted to assimilate to boarding-school life and competed for the football team: "Football began on Monday . . . alas, I tried in vain to get on the team. Still, football is a most delightful game, and I am very sorry I am not on a regular team."[4] Years later, when Harvard sought a donation for its football team, his views had evolved. He retorted that football was "immoral, dangerous, brutal."[5]

At St. Paul's, he also competed for a position on the more sedate cricket team but never made the cut, despite his robust physique. He settled instead as an editor of the student newspaper and hoped it would teach him "to act for myself on my own responsibility. You see, I am very deficient in self-reliance."[6]

During Jack's school years, his father traveled abroad for both business and pleasure, often accompanied by Jack's older sister Louisa. Jack's sisters Louisa, Juliet, and Anne were raised in the tradition of the European aristocracy with tutors in French and German who ensured that they read the classics and learned to sew. The sisters tended to be secluded except for a small circle of family and friends. They were not called upon to perform mundane tasks of housekeeping, laundry, or cooking. They traveled abroad for extended periods, including regular visits to their grandfather's homes in London and Roehampton. There were sojourns in Paris at the Bristol Hotel and cruises down the Nile River wearing haute couture from the House of Worth in Paris.

While his sisters traveled, Jack entered Harvard in 1885. Neither his father nor his paternal grandfather was a college man, and one of his ancestors through his grandmother's line was a founding trustee of Yale University. But perhaps his father chose Harvard. Jack's life did not immediately improve at Harvard.

After his first year, he wrote his mother: "As the time approaches, I feel more and more how entirely I hate Cambridge and everything connected with it."[7] He managed to cope at Harvard with the help of his friends Jim King and his future brother-in-law Ned Grew; both had been his schoolmates at St. Paul's.

Jack's sense of belonging came when he "ran for the Dickey" (Delta Kappa Epsilon or DKE), despite the initiation ordeal. Years before, in 1877, the Harvard chapter of DKE inducted a young Teddy Roosevelt. Jack found a source of entertainment in regattas. It all started when he won a betting pool on a boat race, and this forever cemented his love of speed and sleek movement on the water.

While Jack was at school, he wrote his mother: "Do you think there is any chance of Papa coming up here?"[8] Evidence of visits by Pierpont is scarce and Pierpont saw no reason to make up for his absence by showering money on Jack. He was kept on a shoestring budget and all of his expenditures had to be preapproved. When Jack wanted to join the racquet club, he asked for Papa's approval. He requested seven dollars for tennis shoes and "a new hat for purposes of swellness and as Papa don't want me to get things without permission, may I get one, also some small things, [such] as collars, etc.?"[9] A few years later, in an effort to persuade his father to grant approval of his marriage to Jessie Grew, Jack sent a genealogical chart of the Grew family. How could his father disapprove? Jessie Grew was distantly related to Pierpont's first wife, Amelia Sturgis, known as Memie. Pierpont's first marriage ended tragically. Shortly after their engagement, Memie was racked by a cough, later diagnosed as tuberculosis. She continued to deteriorate, but Pierpont refused to delay or forgo the marriage. He intrepidly worked to save her life with the best lung specialists in Paris. Memie wrote of Pierpont to her mother: "I wish you could see his loving devoted care of me, he spares nothing for my comfort and improvement."[10] She died four months after their marriage.

Three years later, Pierpont married Frances Louisa Tracy, "Fanny," the daughter of a successful New York lawyer. She was taller, heavier, and livelier than Memie. Pierpont was no longer the svelte twenty-three-year-old he was when he married Memie. Along with physical changes, he began to exhibit a mercurial temper. A year after their marriage, Fanny gave birth to their daughter Louisa and, a year and a half later, to a baby boy who went nameless for three weeks until they settled on John Pierpont Morgan Jr., calling him Jack. Fanny had two more children, Juliet and Anne.

Pierpont filled his life with work, consolidating railroads across the country and eventually controlled 165,000 miles of US railroad tracks. His complete transformation of an industry was described as "Morganization." By 1887, the combined firms of Jack's father and his grandfather were valued at $30 million (approximately $1 billion in 2024).

Some business transactions took place on Pierpont's 165-foot steam-powered yacht, the *Corsair.* The yacht provided Pierpont with privacy in a floating venue where he could orchestrate transactions with his guests while sailing up the serene Hudson River. Such a deal became known as a "*Corsair* Compact." But the vessel wasn't reserved only for business affairs. There were unconfirmed rumors of discreet rendezvous with women both on the *Corsair* and abroad. Pierpont craved their companionship and showered them with rare paintings, tapestries, English porcelain, jewelry, a private education for their children, and trust funds. According to Frederick Lewis Allen's book *The Great Pierpont Morgan,* Pierpont crassly spread gold jewelry on a hotel table and told the ladies present, "Now, help yourselves!"[11]

After Pierpont's death, Jack still tried to protect his father's philandering image. In 1940, Jack asked an intermediary to contact the author Virginia Woolf to cajole her to drop from her book *Roger Fry* the sentence, "I knew the answer beforehand—family heirlooms to be offered to Pierpont Morgan still sleeping upstairs in the arms of the elderly and well-preserved Mrs. Douglas."[12]

It was too late. The book was already in print.

CHAPTER 14

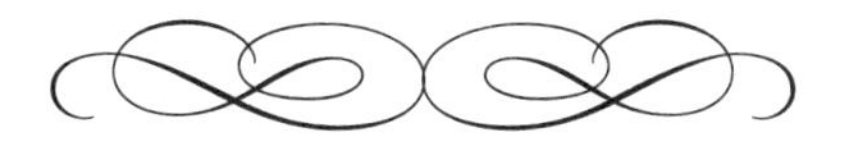

His Return

In 1904, Pierpont, then sixty-seven, summoned his son and his family home from London. They returned on the RMS *Oceanic,* an elegantly furnished luxury liner owned by International Mercantile Marine, a Morgan-owned enterprise.

The staff packed the family's seventy-eight pieces of luggage and boxes of jewelry all valued at $26,000. Arriving in New York, Jack, now thirty-seven, was outraged by the hefty customs duty placed on his personal property purchased in Europe. He broke his long tradition of silence with the press and told them that if he knew about the duty, he would have mailed the packages as it would have been cheaper. When the reporters peppered him with questions about the firm's finances, his father's retirement, and recently created syndicates, Jack had nothing to say. He was a private person working in a private business. He lived by his father's creed: "High finance was the province of a select few, its conduct not subject to public review or government regulation."[1] This philosophy extended to their personal lives as well.

Jack was not privy to his father's plan for him on his return, but Pierpont's plan was for Jack to be close to him. He purchased a brownstone for Jack at 231 Madison Avenue, one house away from his own residence. For the first time in his life, Jack felt wanted by his father. "It is extra nice of Father to let us have it. It will be perfectly charming to be so near 219 and [Louisa at] 225."[2]

Jack's Manhattan home was formidable, boasting forty-five rooms, including twelve bathrooms. Years later, Pierpont would purchase the brownstone in between his home and Jack's, which he razed to make room for a garden adjoining the two homes.

Jack assumed a higher profile at the firm; as the son of the senior partner, he displayed no sense of entitlement at work. He was humble and abhorred flamboyance. He acknowledged his gratitude to Charles Coster, a partner with whom he worked closely. The press reported that Jack acted as the consummate gentleman who never swore and was always respectful of women.

In mid-April 1906, when the San Francisco earthquake turned most of the city to rubble, New York City's Mayor George B. McClellan Jr. named a trusted financier, J. P. Morgan Jr., to serve as treasurer of the earthquake relief fund. The Chamber of Commerce secretary, George Wilson, appointed Jack to another relief fund board.

Pierpont remained the personal embodiment of J. P. Morgan & Co., and Jack continued to live in his father's shadow. It seemed to be more than an odd coincidence that Jack was nowhere to be found when Pierpont assembled bankers to halt the Panic of 1907 and thus avert a complete collapse of the US economy. The *New York Times* reporting on the stock market collapse headlined their article "John Pierpont Morgan A Bank in Human Form."[3] Jack apparently had business to attend to in London.

Jack wrote to his mother: "I wish very much I could have been there to watch and to help in any way I could! But after fifty years of hard work, to have established such a reputation for fair dealing and sound conduct that at a moment of real and great danger the whole country turns to you, [it] must be a real reward for all the years."[4]

Pierpont placed Jack in what he believed would be a perfunctory role as a board member of International Mercantile Marine (IMM), but disaster was imminent. IMM was a company that Pierpont was partially successful in attempting to combine shipping lines. The British placed restrictions on nonnationals owning its shipping lines but, through legal legerdemain, Morgan had a financial interest and engineered for IMM to acquire the White Star Line.

Pierpont asked British CEO Bruce Ismay to serve as managing director of White Star Line. Ismay's family was part of the founders of the shipping line. Each of White Star's ships flew under a British flag. Pierpont's personal enthusiasm for the enterprise was such that he traveled to slip no. 3 in Belfast's shipyard for the launching of the hull of White Star's latest, largest, and most dazzling vessel—the *Titanic.*

In April 1912, one month after sea trials, the *Titanic* set sail out of Southampton on her maiden voyage to New York City with Ismay aboard. Four days after its departure, the *Titanic* began receiving warnings of icebergs. Capt. Edward Smith was undeterred. On April 14, 1912, at approximately 11:45 P.M., an iceberg ripped open the side of the *Titanic* like a can opener. Two hours later, the ship lay under the icy waters of the Atlantic Ocean.

Over fifteen hundred passengers died of hypothermia or drowned. Seven hundred six passengers were saved. The US Coast Guard intercepted a message from a *Titanic* survivor named "Yamsi" aboard the rescue ship, the *Carpathia.* Yamsi was Ismay's crude attempt to disguise his identity by reversing the letters in his name, but he fooled no one.

US senators William Smith and Francis Newlands rushed to New York with the single purpose of making a public display of serving a subpoena on Bruce Ismay, while still onboard the RMS *Carpathia* docked in New York.

Five days after the tragic sinking, Jack, as the Morgan representative on the IMM Board, attended the Senate Commerce Committee's special subcommittee hearings at the Waldorf-Astoria Hotel to hear Bruce Ismay, the first witness, testify.

According to Ismay, "The ship never had been at full speed. I assisted, as best I could, getting the boats out and putting the women and children into the boats. I left the ship in the starboard collapsible lifeboat, which is the last boat to leave the ship, so [as] far as I know there were no passengers left on deck."[5]

Ismay was recalled to testify on two additional days during the thirty-six days of hearings. Over eighty witnesses testified. Some told of ice warnings, inadequate number of lifeboats, the ship's speed, the failure of nearby ships to respond to the *Titanic*'s distress calls, and the treatment of passengers of different classes.

Jack was bitter at what he saw as grandstanding and distortions. He later said, "The investigation of the Titanic has grown from bad to worse. Legislative investigations must be controlled in the future unless Congress wishes to make itself the laughingstock of the world."[6]

The press labeled Ismay a "coward" and blamed Mr. "D'Ismay" for encouraging Captain Smith to increase the vessel's speed and for surviving while others perished.

The Senate's report was issued on May 28, 1912, one month and sixteen days after the *Titanic* sank. The report was an indictment of Ismay, who survived, and Captain Smith, who perished. "On the third day out, ice warnings were received three of the warnings came direct to the commander of the *Titanic* on the day of the accident. No general alarm was sound [*sic*], no whistle blown, and no systematic warning was give [*sic*] the passengers."[7]

The Morgan name, however, was kept out of the Senate's report and largely out of the history of the disaster.

CHAPTER 15

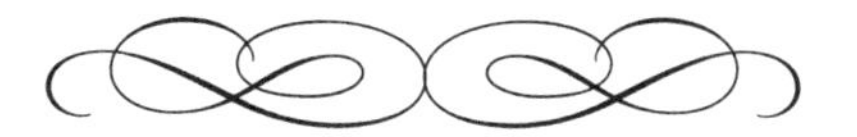

After Morgan, Who?

The public's curiosity about the Morgans was insatiable. The press was happy to accommodate. Pierpont had become the personification of wealth and greed. His girth, height, piercing eyes, and a bulbous nose made him an easy foil for political cartoonists. In contrast, Frank Vanderlip of the National City Bank, the country's largest bank, later known as Citibank, was a nondescript banker of comparative power and wealth, who largely escaped the pen and ink of cartoonists.

Future Supreme Court Justice Louis D. Brandeis, the so-called "people's lawyer," portrayed Pierpont as a ruthless banker and monopolist. He authored *Other People's Money and How Bankers Use It,*[1] which was a compilation of his turn-of-the-century essays published in *Harper's Weekly.* Louis Brandeis waited a year after Pierpont's death to publish the work in which he wrote: "J. P. Morgan & Co., and their associates, held such financial power in at least thirty-two transportation systems, public utility corporations and industrial companies—companies with an aggregate capitalization of $17,273,000,000."[2]

Congressman Charles A. Lindbergh Sr., father of the famed aviator, used Pierpont as a sure way to stir up public opinion against bankers. Lindbergh was determined to bring down Morgan & Co., and said, "I knew that I could not succeed unless I could bring public sentiment to my aid. I had to secure that or fail."[3]

By April 22, 1912, the Louisiana Congressman Arsène Pujo was authorized to form a subcommittee of the House Committee on Banking and Currency to get to the bottom of the "Money Trust," the alleged clique of bankers who were perceived to control the finances of the entire country. The hearings held by the subcommittee were tagged "The Pujo Hearings." Pujo selected Samuel Untermyer, a sharp and successful New York lawyer to lead the investigation. Untermyer was focused on the highest profile name in the banking community—J. Pierpont Morgan.

Jack wrote to his father, who was abroad: "Investigation will probably proceed now on as unpleasant lines as can be arranged."[4] Jack cabled his father that the banking community would not rally around him to form a "united front." They were lying low, intimidated by Untermyer and his committee. Jack believed Untermyer's motive was "based on envy, fundamentally."[5]

The moderately wealthy Untermyer was not just Pierpont's nemesis in the halls of Congress; the two had a history of fierce competition in a world far away from politics and high finance—dog shows.

Pierpont was determined to counter Untermyer's efforts to tarnish his reputation. He hired "the best publicist available."[6]

Untermyer marshalled reams of circumstantial evidence. Bankers held 341 directorships in 112 major American corporations. His theory was a few men, with J. P. Morgan as the leader, formed trusts to merge industries and kill competition.

A photo caught the solemn faces of Pierpont, flanked by his adult children, Jack and Louisa, walking into the Capitol. Pierpont, the banker who saved the market in the Panic of 1907, was now cross-examined on his banking practices.

He exercised maximum self-restraint and was always respectful toward Untermyer and the subcommittee. He described his financial philosophy: "The first thing is character before money or anything else. Money cannot buy it because a man I do not trust could not get money from me on all the bonds in Christendom."[7] He answered each question and did not show signs of buckling to congressional pressure. But those closest to him, including Jack, believed the experience unnerved him. The Morgan honor had been called into question and challenged by politicians and reporters. And Pierpont was the personification of the House of Morgan, the banking community, and industrial giants.

Jack despised the subcommittee's treatment of his father and its hostility toward him. He nicknamed Untermyer "The Beast."

The Pujo hearings never proved the existence of a "Money Trust" per se, but it did shed light on a "community of interests"[8] that concentrated "the control of credit and money in the hands of a few men, of which J. P. Morgan & Co. are the recognized leaders."[9] The publicity of the hearings raised the public's suspicion and distrust of bankers and built support for legislative action. In the end, it proved to be Pierpont's swan song.

Weeks after his appearance before the committee, Pierpont disappeared to Rome and Egypt with his daughter Louisa and her husband.

About a month after he left New York, his doctor issued a cryptic public statement: "[Pierpont Morgan] is not, and has not been, dangerously ill."[10] When Jack sensed that his father might be failing, he contacted his sister Louisa. He was ready to leave for Rome to be with his father.

Louisa gave Jack a blunt and chilling message: "He depends upon your being on the spot in New York. He is too weak [to] make decisions; he wishes [to] leave it [to] you."[11] Privately, Pierpont relinquished control to his son, but he never publicly acknowledged Jack as his successor.

Fifteen days later, from the Grand Hotel in Rome, Louisa's husband, Herbert Satterlee, announced, "Mr. Morgan is dead."[12]

The public announcement came three hours after Jack received a telegram with the news. Jack, his brother-in-law Herbert Satterlee, and a firm partner expressed the view that Pierpont's death was caused or at least accelerated by the stress of the Pujo hearings, which allowed "that little rascal Untermyer [to] smile a happy smile and say, 'I brought it off after all.'"[13]

One newspaper headline read, "J. P. Morgan, King of Finance, Dies in Rome."[14] Sympathy notes and flowers flooded the hotel from the kings of England, Italy, and the German emperor. His Holiness, Pope Pius X, issued this statement: "He was a very great and very good man, I treasured his friendship very much. I am sincerely sorry."[15]

Italian flags were lowered to half-mast on many state and public buildings, and the bells tolled for him at the American Episcopal Church in Rome.

On the day of his death, March 31, 1913, the New York Stock Exchange suspended trading for a ceremonial five minutes and adopted this resolution:

> Resolved, that the death of J. P. Morgan has removed from America's large creative activities its most conspicuously useful figure. To the development of the resources of our country, he has contributed more than

> any man of our day. His immense constructive genius was devoted not merely to American finance and industry, but to the wide field of philanthropy and humanity. The whole world has lost a wise counselor and a helpful friend.[16]

Other resolutions were adopted by the New York Chamber of Commerce, and the American Museum of Natural History, which he helped launch. The Metropolitan Museum of Art placed a life-size portrait of Pierpont at the top of the great main stairway, adorned with a dark-green cypress wreath tied with a knot of mourning veil, in tribute to Pierpont's generosity in donating art to the museum.

Dozens of tributes appeared in the newspapers from bank presidents, high-ranking officers of the armed-forces, members of the judiciary and the Department of Justice.

Former President Theodore Roosevelt, Pierpont's frenemy, wrote: "When he made a promise, he kept it, and untruthfulness and any kind of meanness or smallness alike [were] wholly alien to his character. He was a man that did an enormous amount of good in many ways, which he kept carefully concealed."[17]

An unlikely yet meaningful tribute came from Untermyer, the man who cross-examined him three months prior: "Mr. Morgan was animated by high purposes and he never knowingly abused his almost incredible power."[18]

But Congressman Lindbergh's message was sarcastic and self-serving: "the world's greatest banker—king of bankers—swore that unless he knew the borrowers personally or had an individual knowledge that satisfied him,"[19] he would not lend them money regardless of how "honest the applicants, or how much or how valuable their security. They had to be known to be subservient to that firm."[20]

Jack believed that both Untermyer and Brandeis, who were both Jewish, had a hand in his father's death, and he became more vocal in expressing his anti-Semitic opinions.

Jack arranged for the transport of his father's body from Rome to Paris. In Rome, the streets were lined with residents who removed their hats and bowed their heads as the motorized hearse passed. In Paris, the train was met by the American ambassador, Myron T. Herrick. At the port of Le Havre, the French government ordered full military honors, a tribute usually reserved only for French presidents. A military band played

"La Marseillaise" while the troops saluted Pierpont's casket, which was draped with the French flag.

The casket was placed in the mortuary chapel of the steamer *La France.* It arrived in the New York harbor with her flags flying at half-mast. No photographers were permitted at the pier. Jack and his son Junius climbed aboard the steamer. When the casket emerged, it was draped with an American flag. The ship's orchestra played the "Star-Spangled Banner." The casket was followed by Jack, Junius, Louisa, and her husband, Herbert Satterlee.

On the day of the funeral, the church bells tolled as the Morgan family left their home. Twenty-five thousand New Yorkers choked the streets of Manhattan to either gawk or pay their respects as the car carrying the casket passed on its way to St. George's Episcopal Church. All traffic stopped. Flowers were piled high at the chancel from friends, colleagues, and European emperors, kings and presidents.

Thirty-one social or civic societies attended the services. Among the congregants were the who's who of finance and industry: Andrew Carnegie, Thomas A. Edison, Charles S. Mellon, William K. Vanderbilt Jr., Clarence H. Mackay, August Belmont, Henry C. Frick, George B. Courtelyou, and Frank A. Vanderlip. It was a funeral for the Gilded Aged as much as it was for a single man.

At Westminster Abbey in London, there was a simultaneous funeral service attended by Capt. Sir Walter Campbell, representing King George, and Honorable John Ward, equerry to the king.

At 23 Wall Street, J. P. Morgan & Co. closed its curtains. At the rear of the office sat the vacant swivel chair, behind a rolltop desk, which had belonged to the man who had led the firm for more than forty years.

The Chicago Stock Exchange suspended trading for fifteen minutes during the funeral service.

Pierpont requested burial at the family plot at Cedar Hill Cemetery in Hartford, Connecticut, the city that gave rise to the first successful Morgan, Pierpont's grandfather, who was a founding director of Aetna Insurance.

News outlets speculated on the size of Pierpont's estate and distribution of his assets. Pierpont left his wife, Frances, $1 million and each of his children $3 million. His art treasures were left to Jack with the directive to make them permanently available for the pleasure of the American people at the Metropolitan Museum of Art. Jack received the residuary of Pierpont's estate. Pierpont was never estranged from his daughter Anne, but he loathed her partner, Bessie Marbury, whom he believed "had stolen his daughter, Anne, away from him and prejudiced her against him."[21]

The new forty-six-year-old leader of Morgan & Co., "Jack Morgan" or "Young Morgan," was compared to his father, the "Sphinx of Wall Street." The *Boston Daily Globe* reported on Jack's experience: "up to the present time, he has been that of a staff officer."[22] The *Wichita Eagle* wrote: "For a year, young Morgan attended the directors' meetings, but never opened his mouth except to vote."[23] "If character were the secret of financial influence, as the old man had argued at the Pujo inquiry, perhaps the great days of the Morgan House were over."[24] Within days of the funeral, one newspaper wrote: "It might well be expressed, after Morgan, who?"[25]

Ron Chernow, author of *House of Morgan,* wrote: "What nobody could have foreseen in 1913 was that Jack Morgan—shy, awkward, shambling Jack who had cowered in the corners of Pierpont's life—would preside over an institution of perhaps even larger power than the one ruled by his willful, rambunctious father."[26] During his lifetime, Jack would be featured three times on the cover of *Time* magazine within thirteen years as recognition of his impact on domestic and international affairs.[27] *Time* magazine was one of the most influential news magazines in the early twentieth century.

Part III

Credits Not Loans

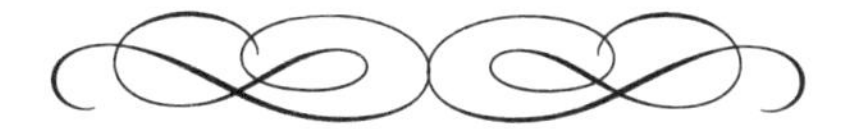

The fact that the Allies found us useful and valued our assistance in their task is the fact that I am most proud of in all my business life of more than 45 years.

J. P. MORGAN

CHAPTER 16

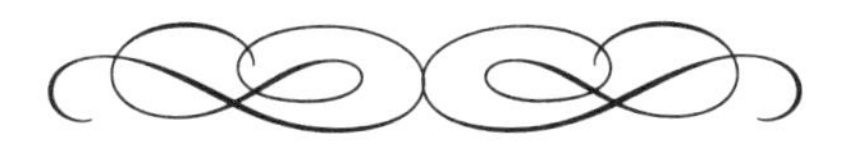

Rational and Measured

On June 28, 1914, gruesome details of the assassination of Archduke Franz Ferdinand, the presumptive heir to the Austrian throne, and his wife, Sophie, were splashed across the pages of the *Ithaca Journal*. An eighteen-year-old Bosnian Serb shot the royals at point-blank range as their motorcade momentarily stopped.

The news dominated most conversations among the Cornell faculty. Frank seemed to have the same keen interest in the news as his colleagues. To everyone around him, including his wife, Frank's life was fulfilled, or so it seemed, by teaching, tutoring, and finalizing a brilliant 232-page thesis, "Goethe Satyros, Shakespeare und die Bibel,"[1] written entirely in German. Leona was busy keeping house, caring for her one-year-old son, Oscar, and preparing for the birth of their second child.

Bad news from Europe was endlessly hurled at news readers. One month after Archduke Ferdinand's death, Austria-Hungry declared war on Serbia. Days later, the German Kaiser told his nation, "Envious peoples everywhere are compelling us to our just defense. The sword is being forced into our hand; we shall restore it to its sheath again with honor."[2] This was the same leader who just a year before had been nominated for the Nobel Peace Prize by the president of the University of California. For the Germans, it was "der Tag"—the long-anticipated day—when they declared war against France and Russia.

Frank's stated position on the war was consistent with that of US President Woodrow Wilson and Secretary of State William Jennings Bryan. Wilson signed a proclamation of American neutrality, and his message was that Americans were to remain "impartial in thought as well as in action."[3] Bryan viewed any perceived breach of neutrality as a violation of US policy and an overt step toward America entering the war. Frank kept any other beliefs he had about the war to himself.

The US economy was in a recession. The European war would limit trade. President Wilson summoned J. P. Morgan to discuss financial matters. After his father's death, he dropped "Jr." Jack was now the man world leaders would look to for advice.

The press wanted a read out of the meeting, but Jack dodged all questions. He managed to squeeze in a private visit to the Senate, where two years before, his father had undergone a cross examination by Untermyer.

The United States wasn't the only country whose economy was in trouble. By the first week of the war, it was reported that France was on the brink of financial insolvency and looking to the United States for support. The French minister of finance, Joseph Noulens, detailed the country's burn rate at about $7 million a day. This was an integral part of the German war plan. The war would end quickly against belligerents who could not afford arms.

Frank, a staunch supporter of neutrality, was infuriated with the news that "Bank of France Opens Credit of $5,000,000 through J. P. Morgan & Co." The *Fatherland,* dedicated to "Fair Play for Germany and Austria-Hungary," headline story was "Mr. Morgan's Proposed Loan to France."[4] German Americans who supported neutrality became incensed.

After his father's death and the Pujo hearings, Jack worked hard to stay under the radar, out of the press, but the European war made that impossible. The newspapers chronicled the ongoing tug-of-war between the administration's neutrality and Jack Morgan's dealings with the Allies. Jack queried the secretary of state about whether the firm could loan money to France and the Rothschilds in London. The answer came back: the government had banned loans to "rival powers." Morgan & Co. had no choice but to abide by those terms.

Jack and the brain trust at the House of Morgan found a way around Wilson's neutrality edict. A complex transaction was structured in which the Bank of France deposited $6 million with Harjes, Morgan & Co. for Americans trapped in Europe. A reciprocal account was opened at Morgan & Co. in New York available to the French ambassador in the United States. The transaction had the appearance of a "wash" and was fully compliant with American neutrality. In reality, it gave the French the ready ability to purchase supplies and munitions in the United States.

The press picked up on the scheme and Morgan & Co. issued the statement: "We have not been asked by the French Government to make a loan but by private interests."[5]

Frank had formulated his opinion that J. P. Morgan was extending the duration of the war by financing the Allies in defiance of the US policy of neutrality.

But the news was now dominated with reports of the August 2 German invasion of Belgium, in violation of the Treaty of London. "Big Bertha"—the massive artillery weapon built by the industrial German company Krupp—pounded Liège, Belgium. Britain declared war against Germany.

A major US campaign sprang up to help the Belgium people. By September 17, Morgan & Co. had collected $30,496 for the Belgium relief fund, of which Jack was a major contributor. Morgan's name was linked over and over with the Allies and that was no surprise. Morgan Grenfell was their London-based firm; Morgan Harjes was the Paris equivalent. Jack and Jessie still owned homes in England.

Frank and others viewed Morgan's purpose in supporting the Allies as rooted in greed. Frank's alignment with US neutrality was in actuality a politically correct means of supporting Germany.

Frank's views were in the mainstream of academic thinking. In September, Frank's Department chairman, Prof. A. B. Faust, wrote an article for the *Fatherland*. "A few weeks ago, the question might well be asked: Is this country neutral, or is it at war? There arose in consequence a huge wave of indignation among the German American citizens throughout the country."[6] Years later, Faust received an honorary degree from the University of Göttingen and gave the Nazi salute to the rector of the university.

Harvard professor Hugo Münsterberg would also weigh in with an opinion. He wrote a protest letter to President Wilson. In his book, *The War and America*, published in September 1914, Münsterberg states that "it is a sin against the spirit of history to denounce Germany as the aggressor."[7] German cruelty to women and civilians, he says, are a myth, "hysteric illusions of overexcited brains."[8]

In September 1914 the chairman of Harvard's German Department, Kuno Francke, wrote a letter to the *New York Times* titled "Goethe v. Elliot."[9] It was a reply to Harvard's president emeritus. He sarcastically paraphrases the president's opinion. "In other words, Germany military and political power is to be crushed in order to set free the German genius for science, literature and art. . . . To advocate for a reduction of Germany to a land of isolated scientists, poets, artists and educators is tantamount to a call for the destruction of the German nation."[10]

The view that Frank and other members of the academy held resonated in middle-class German communities in the United States. In 1914 there were more than eight million German Americans living in the United States, nearly one-tenth of the population. German sympathizers were called "hyphenated Americans."

The largest group of immigrants in New York City were German Americans. In August about three hundred German Americans marched four abreast in New York's Battery Park, carrying German and American flags, chanting, "Hock der Kaiser,"[11] and singing the German national anthem, all within earshot of Morgan & Co.'s temporary office at 15 Broad Street.

There were gatherings in other parts of the country. In Illinois, about 40 percent of the population were born in German-speaking countries. The National German-American Alliance held meetings at the Chicago Auditorium, a popular opera house, which was chosen because it had forty-three hundred seats needed to accommodate the crowd. They demanded that the American press stop ridiculing the Kaiser and treat news from Germany with "greater impartiality." The Germania Club met with representatives from "three score German societies"[12] and the German-Irish alliance to make plans to provide financial support for German war victims.

On September 17, the *Chicago Tribune* supported the German American position with a headline "German Atrocities Fiction, So Far as Tribune Men in Belgium Can Find."[13] Three days later, the newspaper published thirty letters of support from readers. Among them was one from Walter Krembs, the brother of the late Leone Krembs Muenter.

The German-American Society once again denounced J. P. Morgan for supporting the Allies. Ludwig Lore, secretary of the American German Socialist Federation, announced that the Socialist party was arranging demonstrations in large cities, protesting any loan to France. The afternoon edition of the *Staats-Zeitung*, the most widely read German-language newspaper in the United States, was naming Morgan & Co.: "News to the effect that the French government seeks a war loan from J. P. Morgan & Co. has called forth a storm of indignation."[14]

Jack, who detested publicity, was now at the center of the news and worse yet, so was his family. The *New York Times* reported that Jessie had sailed with her daughters to England on July 18. They would be at their country home, Wall Hall, for their annual vacation. As the war escalated, Jessie became terrified at the thought that the Germans would invade England. Jack could not leave New York. Traveling by sea was not a safe option once Germany began using its U-boats. Jack cabled Jessie and told her to stay at Wall Hall with the children until he could secure safe passage for them. Jessie bought a Morris Oxford car so that her daughters could learn to drive for a quick getaway if necessary. Wall Hall's garage became a makeshift hospital for wounded English soldiers, and Jessie and her daughters volunteered at the British Red Cross for several weeks. A safe return to the United States would not occur until October 9, 1914.

Frank believed that the continuation of the war was at the heart of the worldwide financial crisis. The stock markets in Europe virtually ceased operations, and within days there had been a sudden 6 percent decline in share value on the New York Stock Exchange. It was at the offices of Morgan & Co. that the New York City bank financiers would meet and opine on whether the stock market should close. Some had been present for the Panic of 1907.

Their decision was "There is absolutely no reason for closing the Stock Exchange as long as there are buyers."[15] The financiers' recommendation was ignored by the Exchange Board of Governors, who shut down the market until December 12, 1914, longer than any other closing in its history.

This caused an uproar in the German American community. The *Fatherland* provided a more balanced article by Irish playwright George Bernard Shaw, warning of the power of Russia and England under the thumb of the Stock Exchange.

There was some good news, at least within the Holt family. Leona Sensabaugh Holt gave birth to a baby girl on September 13, 1914. She was named Daisy after Leona's stepmother. Both mother and baby were healthy.

Frank purchased two convertible life insurance policies. On the insurance applications, he listed his birthplace as Wisconsin. He insisted that the cover sheet of the policies not include personal information from his application.

And there was more good news. Frank's thesis was accepted and Cornell would confer a PhD at the end of the academic year.

With Frank no longer burdened with his thesis, Leona assumed he would spend more time with the family. That was not the case. Other pursuits would soon occupy Frank.

CHAPTER 17

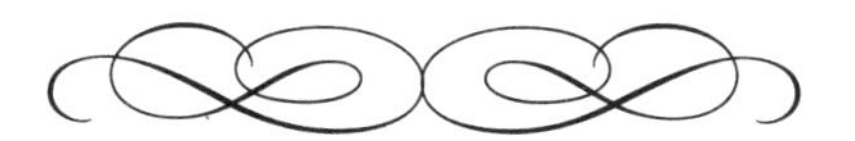

A Long Letter

The subdued Holt family blended well into the Cornell community. Leona was the young loving wife who cared for the couple's son and daughter, and Frank was the erudite, hardworking scholar. Leona supported her husband in his every endeavor, except she held fast to her own religious beliefs. Leona was a member of the Methodist church in Ithaca, and Frank did not affiliate with any church. In conversations with friends, he expressed strong leanings toward Christian Science.

Frank taught his class and tutored students. He often left home early in the morning and would not return until late at night. Leona would never dare question him as to his whereabouts or why he needed to be away from home and the family.

Frank undoubtedly read news coming from the Wilson administration with grave concern. Its neutrality policy was showing signs of fissures. Robert Lansing, counsel to the secretary of state and an expert on international law, remarked that there were "slaughter fields of poor little Belgium."[1] Both Secretary of State Bryan and President Wilson relied on Lansing's expertise. Lansing was holding private meetings with the British ambassador, Sir Cecil Spring Rice, a friend of Jack Morgan. Lansing convinced President Wilson to loosen his neutrality policy and state that private individuals selling any product, including arms, to belligerent nations was "neither unlawful nor unneutral, nor within the power of the Executive to prevent or control."[2] The policy allowed for so-called credits, thinly disguised loans, that clearly would favor the Allies.

Wilson's neutrality policy never precluded a belligerent from buying war munitions from an American company with hard currency. The credit system afforded the British, French, and theoretically the Germans to buy munitions with credit from a US third party such as Morgan & Co.

Jack Morgan immediately took advantage of this new policy. It was reported he established a relationship with the Anglo-French Financial Committee in London. And more Morgan money flowed out to France by way of a $1.5 billion credit.

Other banks followed Jack's lead. Within days, the vice president of National City Bank convinced Lansing to consider short-term bank credits to the Allies, arguing the necessity of the sale of American goods to avoid losing the foreign trade.

But the House of Morgan went one step further and received the designation as purchasing agent for the British and French, earning a 1 percent commission on top of interest payments.

In November, out of utter frustration, Frank penned a long letter to the editor of the *Ithaca Journal.* He was more forthright about his support for Germany and more critical of the paper's anti-German bias. He questioned why the paper, like most of the American press, reported exaggerated accounts of German soldiers' atrocities. The only possible motivation, he concluded, was to encourage contributions to the Belgian Relief Fund. He questioned why the paper failed to report on cruelties practiced upon German troops by the Belgian population, such as Belgians disguising themselves as Red Cross volunteers and then shooting German soldiers. The press, he said, refused to chronicle how the Belgians "invited [German] troops to stay overnight with them and then either poisoned them or killed them while asleep or poured boiling water on them, or cut off their hands, or gouged their eyes out etc., etc. Germany had to protect herself." Frank characterized the Allies, Great Britain, France, and Russia, and the Central Powers, Germany Austria, Hungary, Bulgaria, and the Ottoman Empire as "contestants" and the United States, the neutrals, as "angels of peace." He urged the press to cool its inflammatory rhetoric and view the war as a "quarrel." America, he said, should "act with self-control."[3]

In several conversations with colleagues, Frank expressed his disagreement with the Wilson administration's change in policy and the greed that was driving the banking community.

In November 1914, however, Frank's writing campaign about the war took a backseat when he was forced to confront his past.

CHAPTER 18

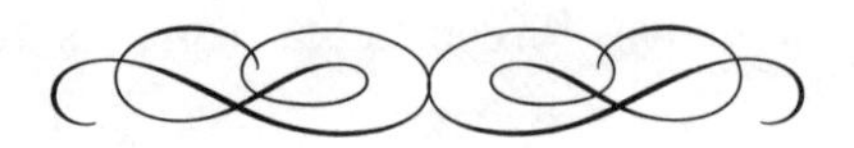

Let Well Enough Alone

Maybe he wouldn't be recognized. After all, it had been more than ten years. But if Frank *was* recognized, would the visitor choose to stay silent? Or would life as Frank knew it end? If Frank was nervous, no one noticed. Although he continued to discuss the war, he was preoccupied with a more pressing concern.

Cornell invited Chester Nathan Gould, a professor in the Germanic Studies Department of the University of Chicago, to work on the Daniel Willard Fiske collection of Icelandic literature.

Erich Muenter and Chester Gould were contemporaries as students at the University of Chicago in the 1890s. They both pursued academic careers but at different institutions. In April 1906, members of the Germanic Studies Department had been buzzing with news of a scandal relating to one of their former students. The news reports told of a young mother poisoned by her Harvard professor husband, a graduate of the University of Chicago. Gould was one of the colleagues who met at the Quadrangle Club of the university to try and quiet the reporters. After the meeting, there was a consensus that Erich disappeared because of the tragic death of his wife and her refusal of medical care.

Weeks later Gould received the fourteen-page typed rant titled "Sensation! Scandal! Autopsy Cremation Assfixiation."[1] The wild story that told of the exploits of "Professor Smith" was undoubtedly written by

Erich. The diatribe made for scary fiction authored by an unbalanced mind but perhaps that had been the point.

In November 1914 a Cornell faculty member introduced the visiting Professor Gould to Frank Holt. Gould paid little attention, but Frank engaged Gould and asked about two professors at the University of Chicago. Frank's bold inquiry may have been born of confidence in Gould's discretion based on his support of him in 1906. At first Gould was puzzled by Frank's knowledge of his institution's faculty. Erich's hair was now streaked with gray and the lines in his face were deeper. He no longer sported his trademark beard.

Gould, like Frank, was an expert in languages and observed that Frank's strange speech patterns varied between a lisp and a foreign accent. Had his Southern drawl disappeared? Finally, Gould, to test or confirm his suspicion of Holt, asked how he knew the Chicago faculty. Frank retreated from his bold step by responding that he merely had heard of their academic success. Gould did not pursue questioning him.

The next meeting occurred days later.

"Hello Gould," Frank said, now greeting him as if they were long-ago acquaintances reunited. When Frank walked away with his loose-jointed walk, Gould's "mental associations began to work, and [he] said, 'I know who it is. It is Muenter.'"[2]

Gould said, "He never avoided me except on one occasion when I saw him with his wife and family."[3]

He decided not to expose Frank Holt's true identity, later stating, "I felt morally justified in running the personal risk, so far as I was concerned, of leaving an erratic individual at large and permitting him to keep on making good. I didn't mention the fact to Frank that I knew him to be Muenter, he did not let on for an instant that he was other than Professor Frank Holt, and yet he knew that I knew he was Muenter. There was something very strange about our talk."[4]

Despite their odd interactions, Gould continued to keep Frank's secret. "As he seemed to be getting along so nicely, and I thought it was better to let well enough alone,"[5] Gould explained. He eventually adopted a widely accepted theory that Erich's behavior was indicative of an unbalanced mind due to overwork.

For now, Frank Holt's identity was safe.

The Gould encounter undoubtedly restored any dip in Frank's confidence. He approached a Cornell faculty colleague in the Latin Department, Charles Bennett, about forming a chapter of the Acacia fraternity, a national organization with the modest objective of virtue, knowledge, and truth. He also asked about joining the Masons. Bennett turned him down on both counts. He looked up Frank's academic background and found his educational experience to be oddly vague. Then he spoke to Gould and was informed that Holt was an assumed name. But it didn't seem to matter. Bennett, like Gould, was not interested in injecting himself into the affairs of a promising scholar and family man, even one who had been suspected of murder. But he drew the line as to the two fraternal organizations and refused to help Holt. Among faculty, there seemed to be a code of silence or, more likely, indifference.

January was the beginning of Frank's last semester at Cornell. Cornell had not offered him a full-time faculty position. Frank had to plan for his future. He finally had his PhD. He had a wife and two children. It was logical that employment was first and foremost on his mind, yet the war dominated his thoughts.

The European war had now claimed six million lives. And the name that continued at the forefront of funding for the Allies was Morgan & Co. It was the sole purchasing agent for Britain and France, ran an operation of experienced executives to choose suppliers, negotiate contracts, purchase heavy artillery, propellants, chemicals, food, and livestock on a line of credit. Jack's affiliation with Britain was so close that his mail was exempted from war censorship, and he was given the code name "Chargeless." Like his father, Jack had become the personal embodiment of the firm.

News within Frank's department at Cornell caught his immediate attention. In February, members of the Cornell faculty invited Harvard's Prof. Kuno Francke to the campus for a ten-day visit. Francke was the chairman of the German Department of Harvard in 1906 when Erich Muenter was a German instructor. At a time when police across the country were still searching for Erich Muenter, Francke's position was that Erich was innocent until proven guilty. But Francke felt strongly that Erich should come forward and defend himself. Francke and Gould were not of the same mindset. This time Frank instinctively sensed a threat.

Frank's only sure option was to leave the campus at once. It would be a difficult request to make of his department chairman Dr. Faust in mid-semester. His reasons needed to be compelling and urgent. He gave two: first, an appointment with a Manhattan-based surgeon regarding back surgery, and second, that he would meet with the soon-to-be president of Southern Methodist University regarding a faculty appointment. SMU, located in the heart of Dallas, would open its doors in the fall of 1915. Chairman Faust believed the request should have come weeks in advance, but it was impossible to deny such an urgent and convincing plea.

Frank had no intention of returning to Cornell until Francke left the campus. When he arrived in New York City, it had already become a hotbed for German undercover operatives. The operatives had one objective—stop the United States from supporting the Allies. The New York German spymaster who controlled the pier division, the special detail division, and the *Geheimdienst,* was Paul Koenig, "PK," known as the "bullheaded Westphalian."[6] PK went by at least a dozen aliases and mandated his operatives do the same. He recruited and offered money to those dedicated to the Fatherland and who would sabotage operations.

When Frank was in New York City, his whereabouts and activities were unknown.

Upon his return to Cornell, after Prof. Kuno Francke left, Frank reported to Chairman Faust that, fortunately, he did not require the surgery nor did he meet with the future president of SMU. He gave no explanation for his delayed return.

With only months to go on his final semester at Cornell, Frank was now more cautious and his activities more clandestine. Leona prayed that Frank would secure a full-time position at SMU. She may have recruited her father to intervene. Reverend Sensabaugh hobnobbed with others who had influence within the Dallas and Ft. Worth communities and shared common religious backgrounds. One such person was Judge Joseph E. Cockrell, a founder of SMU and a voting member of its council.

SMU needed to find faculty to support their rigorous academic programs. Reverend Sensabaugh was present at a meeting which discussed proposed faculty appointments. A Department notation was made next to Frank's name: "Splendid endorsements in the file."[7] On April 13, 1915, the *Ft. Worth-Record Telegram* announced in their paper that "Dr. Frank Holt, Ph.D. from Cornell University and now a teacher there will have charge of French."[8]

The appointment must have made Leona ecstatic. After moving through four states in five years, she, Frank, Oscar, and Daisy would be reunited with her family. She would return with great honor as the wife of a husband she adored, who held a PhD from one of the nation's Ivy League universities. Dallas then had a population of just over nine thousand, and the wife of a university departmental chairman would be viewed as a woman of stature. On the home front, her two children would be showered with love from a grandfather, grandmother, aunts, and uncles. There were so many possibilities in the future. The reverend purchased two lots in University Park for a home for the Holt family.

Frank no longer discussed the war with his colleagues or anyone else. He was tight-lipped despite the news of war supplies purchased in America that continued to pour into England and France financed by credits furnished by American bankers. All was quiet but not for long.

On May 7 the American public learned that a German U-boat torpedoed and sunk the Cunard Lines passenger ship RMS *Lusitania.* The *Lusitania* was about ten miles away from the Irish city with the very English name of Queenstown. Over one thousand passengers died, including 128 Americans. The public was outraged and anguished.

The press was able to garner a quote from Jack and Jessie Morgan while they were aboard the ship *St. Louis:* "I am overcome with horror of it. The details are appalling."[9]

On June 11, President Wilson rejected Germany's claim that it was justified because the *Lusitania* carried "contraband of war." Even if the German allegation was correct, he saw no need for torpedoing a passenger ship and causing the death of innocent Americans. The British and American view was that the sinking was a wartime atrocity. If the ship was carrying munitions as the Germans claimed, the US Supreme Court, in an ancient 1815 opinion, recognized that there was a full and perfect right to "capture enemy goods and articles going to their enemy, which are contraband of war,"[10] but this did not confer the right to blow up the ship and kill innocents.

Frank was mute. He announced to the Cornell faculty in May that he had accepted the chairman's position at SMU. He packed up Leona, two-year-old Oscar, and eight-month-old Daisy, withdrew $600 for Leona, and sent the three of them home to Texas. He told Leona he would meet her in Texas after he completed his research in the libraries of New York City. He promised to write to her. For the first time since they were married, Leona and Frank were separated. It was somewhat unsettling for Leona to return home without her husband.

He packed a few things before leaving for New York but strangely left his trunk full of papers at Cornell. He closed out his bank account, which had a balance of $500, and paid the premiums on the life insurance policies. His last stop was the post office in Ithaca. All mail was to be forwarded to the Mills Hotel, at Thirty-Sixth Street and Seventh Avenue, New York City.

While traveling with her two small children on the long train ride to Dallas, Leona reflected on her marriage. In a note to Frank on their fifth wedding anniversary, she revealed that she had never really understood him.

All was not as it appeared to be.

CHAPTER 19

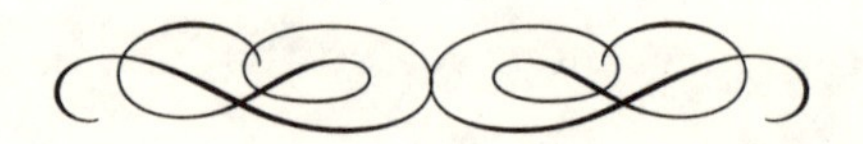

Mills Hotel

Frank Holt signed the register at the Mills Hotel, New York's largest residential hotel for men, as G. W. Holt. Located on Seventh Avenue and Thirty-Six Streets, the Mills Hotel boasted a lobby, sitting rooms, library, restaurant, barbershop, and laundry. Frank paid through the month of June and was given room 1016 on the tenth floor.

Each single room had an electric bulb hanging from the ceiling, opaque windows for privacy, concrete walls, and a "crib-like" bed. For ventilation there was an open transom over the door, through which hallway noise could be heard. In the cold months, the room was heated by a steam coil. At a rate of thirty cents per night, a guest could use a common lavatory located in a center hall and showers in the basement. Towels were scarce and latecomers would find towels "soaking wet unless you were among the first in line."[1]

All hotel guests were required to vacate their rooms between the hours of nine and four to encourage the men to work. The Mills Hotel was particularly popular with German American men since it opened its doors in 1907.

Frank's first task when he arrived was to attend to his mail. He lectured the hotel clerks about the necessity of receiving incoming mail promptly and handling it with special care. On June 8, the day he arrived, six letters were waiting for him. There was a continuous stream of correspondence from Ithaca, Philadelphia, and elsewhere throughout his stay.

He wrote to Leona on a daily basis about his endless hours of tedious research.

Frank did not reveal much to the other hotel patrons. His demeanor was calm and cool and when asked about the hot topic of conversation—the European war—he would only say that the war must end. One guest got under his skin by attempting to engage him on the subject of Morgan's support of the British and French. Frank repeatedly expressed his view that Morgan's funding was the reason the war had escalated, and that Morgan was violating the neutrality policy without consequences. The guest would later tell the press that Frank had threatened to shoot Morgan, which, if true, would have been a serious and uncharacteristic lapse from the tight-lipped academic.

Frank received a telegram from a concerned Professor Faust, chairman of the Language Department at Cornell. Frank had departed the Cornell campus neglecting a sacred academic responsibility—submitting students' final grades on time. Frank quickly responded by providing some grades but carelessly omitted the grades of five or six students. Did he carry his final papers with him or was this imaginative grading of those students' names he could recall? A second exchange of telegrams was necessary to get the remaining grades.

News-watchers eager to get the latest news from the European battlefront gathered around Times Square. Some old timers still referred to Times Square as Longacre Square. Headlines were scrawled on a thirty-foot-high revolving chalkboard and there was also a large canvas with projected news on the *New York Times* building. Frank took time out of his busy day to read the news. One Times Square watcher later claimed that Frank argued with him over war news.

Frank was walking around the streets of Manhattan and feeling at home in the neighborhood known as Kleindeutschland, located near Avenues A and B, which was home to German immigrants.

Kleindeutschland had been devastated in 1904 when over one hundred of its residents, including women and children, boarded the sidewheel steamer *PS General Slocum* for its annual late-spring outing on the East River, organized by St. Mark's Evangelical Lutheran Church. When the *Slocum* caught fire, the passengers leapt from the blazing boat with cork life preservers. The dried-out preservers soaked up the salt water like sponges, causing the passengers to sink slowly and drown.

There had been an outpouring of sympathy and support for the German community from all segments of New York, but by 1915, the tide had turned. The New York press reported on clandestine cells of German saboteurs closer to home who had plans to blow up railroads in New York, New Haven, Hartford, and Connecticut. The SS *Knutsford,* loaded with sugar in the New York harbor, had a bomb hidden in the ship's hold. Other ships seemed to combust spontaneously. And there were reports that operatives communicated through German-owned radio stations such as the one in Sayville, Long Island, and through an offshore Marconi. Americans had also not forgotten the 128 American souls buried at sea when the German U-boat sunk the *Lusitania.*

One paper summed up the country's sentiment of the time. "It was a deed for which a Hun would blush, a Turk be ashamed, and a Barbary pirate apologize. To speak of technicalities and the rules of war in the face of such wholesale murder on the high seas is a waste of time. The law of nations and the law of God have been alike trampled on."[2]

CHAPTER 20

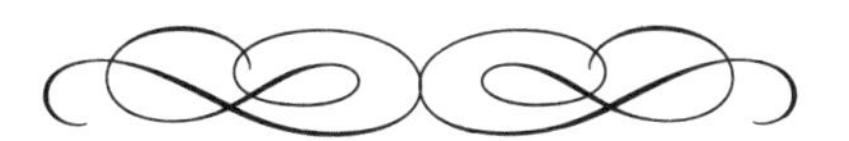

Mr. Totten

Frank was not actually visiting libraries. On Thursday, June 20, he left the Mills Hotel with a traveling case and walked to one of New York's newest and grandest structures, Pennsylvania Station. He boarded the Long Island Railroad for a village then named Central Park, situated about thirty-five miles east of Manhattan's Central Park. The Central Park community was nestled in the present-day areas of Farmingdale and Bethpage, and at the time, was on the edge of the Long Island Pine Barrens. It was a rural, wooded area intersected by the Vanderbilt Motor Parkway, where the thirty-mile Vanderbilt Cup auto races had run.

Frank requested a cottage in a remote part of the village that was beyond sight from the road and hidden by trees. He introduced himself as Mr. Totten and told Lewis Ott, the landlord's liaison, that he wanted to breathe the country air while recuperating and resting and, above all, he did not want to be disturbed. Ott showed him a cottage with two rooms, a spring cot, three chairs, and a small wooden table. Between the rooms was a double-burner oil stove. Totten paid for the months of June and July.

He settled into the cottage with few personal possessions and a plethora of papers.

Within days neighbors complained about Totten to Ott. At night, there were bonfires with the crackle of flames and rising ash filling the night sky. Totten fed reams of paper into the flames, assuring their destruction. He set off explosives daily that neighbors found jarring. Instead of the scent of fresh pine, the air was filled with the smell of cordite and sulfur. And there were the jarring sharp bangs from a makeshift firing range.

Ott said, "He made bonfires nearly every night. Some of these were so large that they made neighbors nervous."[1] When complaints about Totten reached a crescendo, Ott inspected the property and found, in the rear, a high-board fence installed by Totten for marksmanship exercises. Ott implored him to cease his fires, explosions, and limit his target practice. But Ott was inclined toward a mindset that the renter should be given a pass on his behavior. "You know he was a foreigner from the way he spoke, and you expect almost anything from foreigners. He used to practice pistol shooting a whole lot. He would set up targets near his place and shoot and shoot and shoot. Most of this was at two-hundred feet, a distance difficult for most men to shoot with a revolver. I saw some of the targets and, believe me, they looked as though he could shoot some."[2]

Both curious and nosy neighbors watched Totten. He rode the railroad daily from the local station, Central Park, and sometimes walked several miles to use the Syosset station. His routine was to leave with a suitcase that seemed as light as a feather, only to return to the cottage with it visibly weighed down.

On Monday, June 21, Totten left Central Park for Long Island City, Queens, across from Manhattan, where the Aetna Explosives Company was located. He ordered two hundred sticks of dynamite with 40 percent purity. The percentage refers to the amount of nitroglycerin, a highly unstable explosive. The remaining 60 percent were stabilizers used to prevent instant combustion. The dynamite, when exploded, had enough force to clear solid rock formations for roads and mining. More recently it became a weapon of war, and Swedish inventor Alfred Nobel became known as a "Merchant of Death." To secure an honorable legacy, Nobel left the bulk of his fortune for the creation of the eponymous prizes for excellence and to promote fraternity among nations.

Ott watched as Totten brought a heavily loaded motor wagon to the cottage. He couldn't see what was in the wagon because it was covered with bags of grain. The driver, a stranger in the neighborhood, seemed to be an acquaintance of Totten. Ott watched Totten and the driver carry the weighty packages into the cottage, and then the driver drove off.

Three more shipments arrived at the Syosset station for Totten. He would sign the receipt "Mr. Hendricks," sometimes spelling it as "Hendrix."

One trunk, weighing over forty pounds of unknown content, arrived at the rail station by prepaid express on June 22 from J. Wolf & Son in New York.

The next shipment arrived on June 23, a box weighing one hundred pounds from another explosive provider in Long Island City. According to the waybill, it contained one hundred feet of fuse, one hundred No. 6 blasting caps, and one hundred four-foot "explodes." In simple terms, one hundred blasting caps or detonators could be used to trigger one hundred separate explosions.

On June 28, more boxes arrived for Hendricks at the Syosset railroad station. They were shipped from Aetna Explosives Company with the label from Keystone Powder Co. The bill of lading stated that it was two boxes containing 120 pounds of high explosives.

Totten was usually fastidious about picking up the deliveries. But on June 29, he paid for a chauffeur-driven car to pick up the delivery at the Syosset station. The car arrived at five o'clock in the evening and the freight house was closed. When Totten arrived at the station, he panicked. He pleaded with the freight house attendant, Mr. Carnes, to let him pick up his delivery and promised to "never trouble him again."[3]

Mr. Carnes had previously accepted packages for Totten addressed to Hendricks and Hendrix and now realized that they were the same person. Mr. Carnes, a fair man, was sympathetic to the reasonable request. Totten quickly loaded the trunk into the hired automobile's tonneau with great care, and the car immediately drove off. Unknown to the driver, this vehicle was filled with dynamite, caps, and fuses. The little cottage had become an armory.

Part IV

Seven Days in July

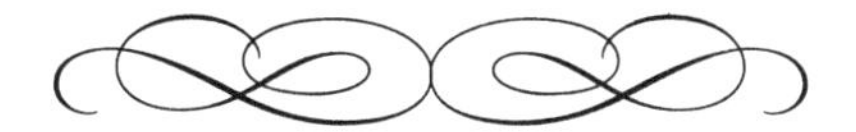

The whole German nation had started out on the war with the cry of "World domination or annihilation" and we recognized that world domination by Germany would bring complete destruction of the liberties of the rest of the world.

J. P. MORGAN

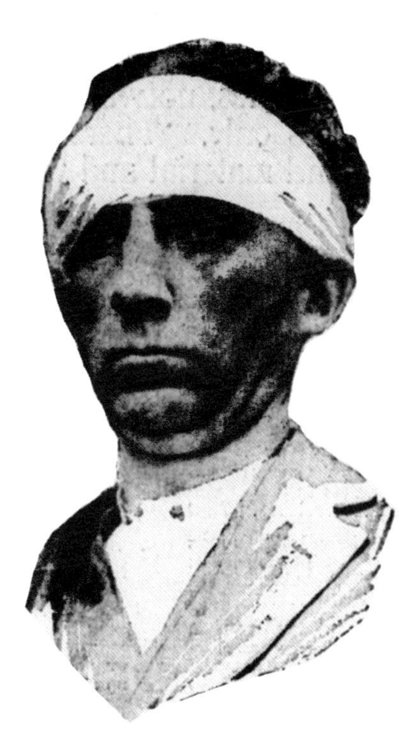

Above left: Erich Muenter, circa 1906 (*Harrisburg Telegraph* [1879–1948], July 7, 1915, from Library of Congress, Chronicling America, Historic American Newspapers)

Above right: Frank Holt, July 3, 1915 (*Harrisburg Telegraph* [1879–1948], July 7, 1915, from Library of Congress, Chronicling America, Historic American Newspapers)

Left: Frank Holt, graduation from Polytechnic College, 1909 (Special Collections & University Archives, Wesleyan University, West Library TX)

Above left: Leone Muenter with daughter Helen, circa 1905 (*The Washington Times* [1902–39], May 13, 1906, from Library of Congress, Chronicling America, Historic American Newspapers)

Above right: Helen and Leone Krembs, circa 1909 (Courtesy of Steve Treanor)

Right: Leona Sensabaugh, graduation from Polytechnic College, 1909 (Special Collections & University Archives, Wesleyan University, West Library TX)

Left to right: Louisa Morgan Satterlee, J. P. Morgan Sr., and J. P. Morgan Jr. entering US Capitol for the Pujo hearings (Library of Congress, Prints & Photographs Division, photographed by Harris & Ewing, LC-DIG-hec-01828)

Matinicock, East Island, Glen Cove, New York (Courtesy of the Glen Cove Public Library, Robert R. Coles Long Island History Collection)

Above: US Capitol senate reception, July 2, 1915 (Library of Congress, Prints & Photographs Division, LC-DIG-npcc-32157)

Left: J. P. Morgan Jr. (Library of Congress, Prints & Photographs Division, LC-DIG-ggbain-19047)

US Capitol senate reception (Courtesy of Architect of the Capitol)

Above: Matinicock, East Island, Glen Cove, New York (Courtesy of the Glen Cove Public Library, Robert R. Coles Long Island History Collection)

Left: Holt in custody (*New York Tribune* [1855–1924], July 4, 1915, from Library of Congress, Chronicling America, Historic American Newspapers)

Judge Luyster's courtroom in Glen Cove (Courtesy of North Shore Historical Museum)

CHAPTER 21

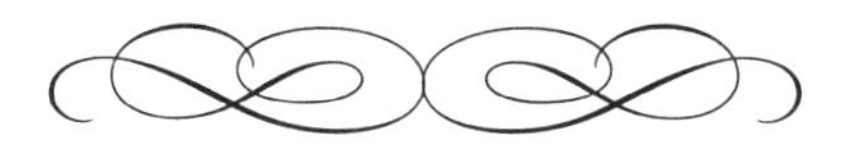

July 1

Dr. Walter T. Scheele

Frank's next mission was the purchase of handguns. New York's recent gun-licensing laws required prospective gun purchasers to wait while their license application was reviewed. This forced Frank across the Hudson River to Hoboken, New Jersey.

Frank walked into John S. Menagh's Hardware store to purchase two revolvers. Menagh had only one to sell, an Iver Johnson .38 caliber revolver. Frank bought it under the name C. Hendricks, with a Syosset address. He then walked to a pawnshop on Grove Street, owned by Joseph Keechen, and purchased a .32 caliber revolver. He wanted each of the sellers to guarantee that the revolvers would fire but neither proprietor was willing to assure performance.

Frank's whereabouts were unknown immediately before or after the purchase of the firearms. But blocks away from the pawnshop at 1133 Clinton Street was the secret laboratory of Dr. Walter T. Scheele, a chemist who had been a German spy for twenty-three years. Scheele had an impressive inventory of explosives, rapidly accelerating incendiary chemicals, and missiles propelled by compressed air. He experimented with instant accelerants and timed incendiary devices that could be used on a tactical level. The devices were no larger than a pencil or cigar. Dr. Scheele not only tested explosives, he provided step-by-step instructions to operatives on how to assemble them.

In Hoboken some eighty ships of the Hamburg-American line lay dormant due to the British embargo. The ships dumped hundreds of unemployed, able-bodied German seamen, all potential recruits for Paul Koenig's spy machine operation.

Frank left Hoboken for Long Island. While seated in a railroad car, he was seen speaking with a "short, thick set"[1] man who carried a large suitcase. The suitcase was so heavy that both men had to lift it onto the baggage rack of the train. Between the Jamaica and New Hyde Park stations, a trip of about fifteen minutes, they changed their seats at least four times. They spoke in whispers, with distinct German accents. A railroad employee noticed their strange behavior. When the train reached Sea Cliff, the village next to Glen Cove, the short man left, taking the heavy suitcase with him. The employee eavesdropped and heard Frank say, "Goodbye and good luck to you. I will see you tomorrow at the same place if you are alive."[2] Contrary to what Frank told Leona about being alone, he knew and met with other like-minded men.

Frank exited the train at the Glen Cove station, fifteen miles away from Central Park. At the station, he hired a car, sat in the front seat, and chatted up the driver Matthew Kramer, asking him to drive slowly toward the Morgan House. Kramer thought nothing of his request; Morgan had many guests. Kramer drove along Dosoris Lane, the road bordering acres of beautiful land on the north shore of Long Island. The car turned onto Danas Highway, which was not a highway but a narrow, winding, steep, downhill road with three forty-five-degree turns, leading to a causeway. The causeway crossed over Dosoris Pond, a 110-acre tidal pond fed by the Long Island Sound. As the car approached the causeway, Frank now had an elevated view north clear across the Long Island Sound about five miles to Rye, New York. At the end of the causeway, on the left, was West Island, later the home of Jack's son Junius. But the car made a sharp right turn onto the 100-foot bridge to East Island.

Frank casually asked Kramer to drive to the Morgan mansion. He didn't get out, but he surveyed and scouted the mansion's entrance before ordering the driver to return to the train station. Kramer found the request odd, but the curious often wanted a glimpse of the famous financier's home. When Frank asked Kramer if he knew Campbell (a Morgan chauffeur), he became suspicious of the stranger. Kramer realized that his passenger was not just another voyeur of the rich and famous but a person who had inside information as to Morgan's staff and possibly more. But Kramer kept this to himself and alerted no one.

Frank returned to his cottage in Central Park. He hired a car to pick him up at 6 A.M. the next morning.

CHAPTER 22

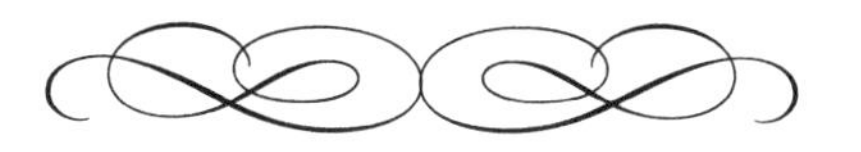

July 2

Pearce

The driver, a willing young man, offered to carry his trunk, but Frank insisted that he heave the heavy trunk onto the wagon himself. When he boarded the train at Central Park, Frank carried only an attaché case. The remaining cases and trunks, filled with explosives, were sent to Pennsylvania Station, where they could be stored in the Baggage and Parcel room for later retrieval by the ticket holder.

The railroad agent, Harry Fredericks, remembered, "He was nervous, I should say, and kept walking up and down the platform as he waited for the train. For want of anything else to do, I spoke to him and asked him what he thought of the War. He looked at me sort of earnest-like as if to make sure I was not kidding him and then spoke up: 'I don't think it is right. Preparedness for war leads to war. It ought to be stopped."[1]

After arriving at Pennsylvania Station, Frank purchased a ticket and boarded the next train to Union Station in Washington, DC, carrying only his attaché case.

Frank sat for a shave before exiting Union Station later that afternoon. He traveled the short distance to a boardinghouse at Delaware Avenue and C Street and checked in under the name Pearce.

July 2 was a steamy eighty-six-degree day in Washington, but Frank wore the customary male attire of the day, a serge jacket.

He walked to the Capitol in the late afternoon, still carrying his attaché case. Visitors could enter the Capitol freely. Since 1898, guests to the Capitol were treated to free guided tours by volunteers, who had provided evidence of good character to the Capitol Police.

Frank climbed the steps of the Capitol into the Rotunda and ambled through the magnificent but empty halls for about thirty minutes. He attempted to open the door of the main Senate chamber, but it was locked. The Senate had been out of session since March and would not return until December.

Then Frank wound his way around the chamber and opened the door to the beautifully appointed Senate Reception Room. The room evoked the look and feel of a salon in a European palace. One half of the room featured a shallow coffered dome, while the northern portion was adorned by a Roman-style vaulted ceiling with gilded floret inserts. A monumental arch divided the room in half. Between the two exterior windows was a fireplace. No expense was spared with frescos, artwork, a crystal chandelier, and imported mosaic floor.

The impressive Senate Reception Room had previously been known as the Ladies' Reception Room or the Ladies' parlor, named for the Civil War widows who lobbied senators for survivor benefits or government employment. When telephone booths were installed in 1893, the room became known as the Public Reception Room, a place where senators and staff could meet with constituents, visitors, and lobbyists before entering the floor of the Senate.

There was one policeman on patrol in the Senate wing, and he was making his rounds in the Rotunda. The only other person on the Senate side was Jones, a Capitol guard who checked the Reception Room ten minutes before Frank entered.

Frank opened his attaché case. There it was, the small device built with exceptional precision. The assembly and execution of timed explosives posed a great danger to the builder. This bomb had a timer. A lit fuse was too unreliable and would leave insufficient time for a comfortable escape through the labyrinth of corridors. He stashed the device near the telephone booths so that it would not be detected by the guard.

Frank walked out of the Capitol and wandered the streets of Washington. As planned, it would be hours of waiting for the sound of his success. There was no guarantee that the timed explosive would ignite, but he had confidence in the device.

He mailed a letter to President Wilson, signed by Pearce, explaining his purpose and intent in targeting the Capitol, which was to call attention to "the murders being done in Europe by American ammunition."[2] He mailed four more previously typed letters to Washington newspapers. The letters were dated June 1 and rambled on about ending the sale of arms to the Allies. He inserted, by hand, the word *senate* next to the word *room* as a last-minute addition confirming the exact place where the bomb was located. The letters were typed on three different typewriters, with three different postscripts, but all were signed Pearce. It was 10 P.M., six hours after Frank entered the Capitol, and still no explosion. He had no other mission but to wait.

And then, at 11:23 P.M., there was a thunderous roar that caused the Capitol to tremble. Chaos, fear, and shock descended on the residents who ran out into the street toward the deafening blast. They witnessed shards of glass from the blown-out windows of the Reception Room and realized that someone bombed the Capitol. The Senate Reception Room was blown to pieces.

Jones, a Capitol guard, was seated on the floor beneath the Reception Room and was said to be lifted from his chair by the force of the explosion. Watchmen at the far end of the Capitol, a city block away, believed the Capitol dome had collapsed.

The explosion blew a hole that measured one foot in diameter and three inches deep in the brick inner lining of the marble walls under the shattered window. The marble wall on one side of the room had a four-foot crack. The swinging door of the District Committee Room was untouched, but the transom was blown out. The squares of glass in the roof of the anteroom were nearly all destroyed. Tops were torn off the telephone booths. An onyx clock that had sat on a mantle, a fixture for the past twenty years, was covered in black soot, with its hands frozen at 11:23. The heavy plate-glass mirror over the mantle was reduced to a pile of shards, and the locked door at one side of the room, about twenty-five feet away, was blasted open. This door led into another room, where the pendeloques were blown off chandeliers. A heavy mahogany panel was ripped from a section of the door leading into the sergeant-at-arms office on the east side of the room. Plate glass was broken in the lobby outside the bronze doors of the Senate wing. Flying fragments of glass nicked oil portraits. There were piles of shattered plaster from the ceiling fresco, painted by Constantino Brumidi, and mirror shards and splintered woodwork littered the richly patterned Minton tile floor. Small fragments of iron, brass, and steel were scattered throughout the room.

This was the first attack on the United States Capitol since the War of 1812, when, on August 24, 1814, the Corps of Royal Engineers, under the command of Captain Blanchard, set it on fire. In the 1814 attack, the Senate wing was reduced to rubble.

Frank walked to Union Station and boarded the midnight train to New York City. His attaché case was somewhat lighter than when he arrived.

CHAPTER 23

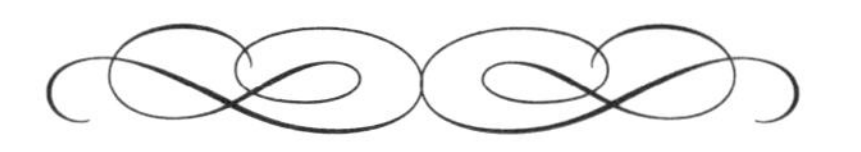

July 3

Thomas C. Lester

The train pulled into Pennsylvania Station just before six o'clock on Saturday morning. Frank mailed a letter to Leona and then boarded the Long Island Railroad to his next stop—the home of J. P. Morgan.

The morning air was cool when Frank disembarked from the train at the Glen Cove station, looking like summer with a Panama hat, light trousers, and a blue serge jacket. Almost imperceptible was a plain gold clasp pin with "09" engraved on it fastened to his cravat, which he wore proudly commemorating the year of his graduation from Polytechnic College. He walked over to the taxi stand, hired a car, and directed the driver, Fred Ford, to take him to the Morgan estate.

On this day, the Morgan estate was buzzing with preparations for a special family event.

Mr. Morgan's reputation among the locals was that of an authentic, honest, fair-minded gentleman. Those he employed were loyal to him. The Morgans kept a low profile and the location of Matinicock was no secret to the locals. No guards and no gates were needed on East Island.

This July morning, Jack, Jessie, British ambassador Sir Cecil, and his wife Florence were in the breakfast room. Sir Cecil's not-so-secret agenda was to wring as much financial support as he could for Great Britain from the House of Morgan. But Sir Cecil's plan did not dampen the air of celebration in the Morgan house. Attention had been paid to details so that the Morgans' eldest son, Junius, and his bride could enjoy the day with family and friends.

Frank instructed his driver, "We may meet Mr. Morgan's automobile along the way. If we do I want to throw my suitcase in Mr. Morgan's car and I'll jump in myself."[1] Ford had to wonder who his passenger was. The driver, of course, was not privy to the financier's friends or acquaintances. He drove along Dosoris Lane, down the steep winding Danas Highway, over the causeway and the bridge to the Morgan estate. Frank paid the fare, took his case, and Ford drove off. Surreptitiously, Frank threw the suitcase into a hedge before walking to the front door.

When he rang the doorbell at 8:57 A.M. Jack's butler, Stanley Cecil Physick, answered.

"I want to see Mr. Morgan," He handed the butler his card: "Society Summer Directory. Represented by Thomas C. Lester."

"What is your business with him?"[2]

"I can't discuss that with you. I am an old friend of Mr. Morgan. He will see me."[3]

But Physick resisted. "You must tell me the business you have with him."[4]

Then the visitor pulled both hands out of his pockets, holding a revolver in each one. He shoved the guns into the butler's ribs, pushing him into the house. "Don't dare try to stop me."[5] Instantly, Physick knew that his life was in imminent danger and so was Mr. Morgan's. He quickly devised a subterfuge.

Physick was a loyal employee who would continue in Morgan's service for thirty-four years. He started as a footman and rose to become the butler, head of the household staff. He was a patriot and later founded the Butlers' Committee of New York, supporting the government's effort with a "Food Will Win the War" program, which committed domestics to "Meatless Monday" and "Wheatless Wednesday."

Following the gunman's order, Physick led him into the foyer of the house. He walked the intruder down the hallway, to the left of the large, central staircase and pointed to the end of the hall. "You will find Mr. Morgan in the library."[6] The library was located at the northeast end of the house, the end furthest from the breakfast room. The intruder opened each door along the extended hallway.

Physick then sprinted back down the hall to the right side of the staircase, in the direction of the northwest breakfast room, and shouted, "Take the backstairs, Mr. Morgan, upstairs, Mr. Morgan!"[7]

When Jack heard Physick's shouting, he immediately followed his directive and ran up to the second floor via a back staircase that was out of sight of the library. Jessie followed.

Jack and Jessie reached the second floor. They were bewildered. What caused Physick to alarm them? The first person they encountered on the second floor was Miss Rosalie McCabe, the Irish nanny. She stepped out of one of the rooms when she heard Mr. Morgan's voice asking, "What has gone wrong up here? What do you want me for?"[8]

"Nothing has happened up here that I know of. Everything has been quiet," Rosalie said.[9]

Jack and Jessie went from room to room, searching for the source of the trouble.

When Rosalie stepped into the center hallway, she looked down the grand staircase. There was the gunman charging up the stairs. She screeched, "He's coming upstairs."[10]

Jessie then rushed to the top of the stairs. She stood between the invader and her husband. Jack pushed Jessie aside.

The two men were eye to eye. The gunman pointed both revolvers at Jack and shouted, "So you are Mr. Morgan. Now, Mr. Morgan, I have got you."[11]

Then without a second's delay, the forty-eight-year-old financier hurled his more than two hundred pounds on the gunman, toppling him to the floor of the landing. The intruder was pinned beneath Jack. He jabbed one gun into Jack's body and pulled the trigger, firing two shots. The sound echoed through the center hall of the mansion. In the fight between the two men, there were two additional clicks of the hammer, but the revolver did not discharge. Jack didn't flinch. An unyielding Jack wrestled the gunman until he could grab his wrist and shake the revolver out of his right hand. One gun dropped to the floor. The gunman's left hand gripped the second revolver tightly. It was stuck under Morgan's body. The gunman struggled to free his left hand holding the revolver. Jessie, who refused to leave her husband while he was under attack, seized the opportunity to wrench the gun out of the gunman's left hand.

Physick had gone downstairs to summon help from the staff. Now he ran up the stairs, holding a large piece of anthracite coal, which is hard and brittle. He found the intruder still pinned under Jack's body and slammed the coal onto his forehead. The stunned gunman was immobilized. The other staff members landed punches and then tied him up. Finally, the would-be assassin was subdued. Jack stumbled to his feet and left the immediate area. Jack's staff carried the deadly intruder out to the front lawn and held him until the authorities arrived.

Jack blurted out that he had been shot. Jessie had not realized that bullets had entered her husband's body. She was hysterical. In an attempt to calm his wife, Jack assured her he was not seriously hurt, was not in pain, and that his injuries were only slight, an opinion that was not entirely shared by the doctor who treated him. Jack calmly telephoned Dr. William H. Zabriskie, who lived three miles away on Highland Road and requested his assistance.

The police apprehended the gunman and drove him with the now discovered suitcase to the Town of Oyster Bay Courthouse on Glen Street, less than three miles away. Jack watched through a window.

At 10:40 A.M., the following statement was issued by the Manhattan office of J. P. Morgan & Co.: "J. P. Morgan was shot by an unknown man, presumably a crank, at 9 o'clock this morning at his home in Glen Cove. His physicians advise that his wounds are not serious."[12]

The doctor determined that one bullet hit Jack's thigh and exited the back of his leg. The second bullet entered the right quadrant of his abdomen. After the examination, Dr. Zabriskie contacted Morgan's Manhattan physicians, Dr. Lyle and Dr. Marcoe. The bullet in the abdomen presented a serious condition.

Jack was ordered to bed but refused until he telephoned his mother to allay her fears before the news was broadcast to the world. Sir Cecil used his best efforts to keep the Morgan children calm.

Later that day, a household staff member found a stick of dynamite on the front lawn.

At 11:30 A.M., Jessie, now somewhat more composed, sent the following telegram to Jack's mother: "Jack attacked by a lunatic this morning. Slightly wounded. Doing well. JESSIE"[13]

Within minutes, local newspaper men swarmed Matinicock. The staff would only say that Mr. Morgan had been shot twice and the wounds were not life threatening. A physician's report of Mr. Morgan's condition would be announced at noon.

For the first time, a guard was posted at the bridge to East Island.

To the residents of Glen Cove the troubling news of a Capitol bombing had grabbed their attention but presented no immediate danger. Now they were buzzing about the assassination attempt on Morgan's life right in their own community. The police phoned the local judge, prosecutor, constables, and a physician asking that they immediately go to the Glen Cove Courthouse. Physick, taxi drivers, and other witnesses were brought to the courthouse for questioning. The essence of the press dispatches was that J. P. Morgan was shot, his condition was unknown, and the assailant was taken into custody.

Glen Cove became the center of all news. Never in its history had there been such a momentous event. The quaint community with its miles of beaches, harbor, and Long Island Sound was home to ten thousand people, a handful of whom were wealthy and the balance hard-working merchants and laborers. An electric trolley connected the harbor with the downtown area. There was a public library, a vaudeville, and movie theater. It was an idyllic location for summer homes because it was an easy jaunt by car or train, just thirty miles from New York City.

Curious locals and the press were jamming the street trying to enter the one-room courthouse. The overflow crowd stood outside.

The assailant was escorted into the redbrick courthouse built in 1907. The facade was a Dutch Colonial–style building with a sloping green-tile roof. The interior of the building evokes the feeling of a country church rather than a one-room courthouse with its nineteen-foot ceiling. The judge's chambers are in the rear and a prison cell in the basement. (Today the courthouse, now a museum, stands exactly as it did in 1915.) The would-be-assassin was ushered down to the basement into the cell, a room seven-by-fifteen feet with a cot.

News traveled quickly and statements of concern and good wishes for J. P. Morgan came from near and far. New York City Mayor John Purroy Mitchell, an anti-Tammany reform politician, remarked that the assault on Mr. Morgan was a "deplorable occurrence. I have a very high opinion of Mr. Morgan as a man and as a citizen."[14] A year before, Mitchell had also been the target of an assassination attempt. The bullet missed its mark and hit a pedestrian. Mitchell would die in the closing months of World War I on an air-training mission. An air base on Long Island would be named in his honor.

Others sent messages of concern and hope, including from the president of National City Bank, senators, and congressmen. President Wilson learned of the attempt on Morgan's life and said he had known Mr. Morgan for some time and was glad to hear that his wounds were not serious.

Dr. J. S. Connolly arrived first at the courthouse. He examined the prisoner. He had a deep gash over his eye. The doctor dressed and wrapped his wounded head. He determined there was no need for him to be hospitalized or the proceedings delayed.

Constable Frank McCahill filed a felonious assault charge against the nameless defendant. The Honorable William E. Luyster lived only minutes away in Glen Cove and rushed over to the courthouse. The forty-two-year-old was elected justice of the peace for the town of Oyster Bay and would preside over the arraignment.

When the police attempted to ascertain biographical information from the assailant—name, address, date of birth, occupation—the prisoner was reticent and refused to answer.

The police delivered the prisoner's possessions and his jacket to Judge Luyster and Constable McCahill. When they opened the perpetrator's suitcase, they were astounded by what they saw—two foot-long dynamite sticks labeled "KEYSTONE POWDER COMPANY, SIXTY PER CENT. EMPORIUM, PA.," a bottle of nitroglycerine, and a number of loose cartridges. This was no ordinary crank. This man had the capability of inflicting mass destruction. The prisoner's portable bomb kit presented an immediate danger.

In the pocket of his jacket was a dynamite stick. In the other was "pocket litter," a cartoon from the *Philadelphia Record,* dated July 1, 1915, with the caption "Dangerous Fireworks," and a drawing of a female bearing a sash emblazoned with "Columbia"[15] reaching into a box filled with war munitions and pushing Uncle Sam away. Uncle Sam represented the policy of strict neutrality being pushed away by the craven interests of some segments of the American public represented by Columbia. The pocket also contained four ten-dollar bills, an express company receipt, several local railroad tickets from Texas and northwestern locations, and a paper with the names of Jack Morgan's four children. In another pocket there was the sailing schedule of the International Mercantile Marine (IMM) vessels with a pencil mark next to the name of one of the ships.

News of the assassination attempt and the dynamite whirred through the telegraph wires at the headquarters of the New York Police Commissioner Arthur Woods, Jack Morgan's nephew-in-law. Woods immediately dispatched the captain of the Bomb Squad, Thomas J. Tunney, a twenty-three-year veteran of the force. Tunney had become an expert on German spy operations.

Woods originally created the first Bomb Squad a year before when a bomb intended for John D. Rockefeller exploded in a Harlem apartment building, destroying three floors and killing three conspirators and one innocent victim. Two months later, a bomb was detonated in the northwest corner of St. Patrick's Cathedral, sending iron shrapnel flying, shattering a stained-glass window, and blowing an eighteen-inch hole in the floor. Another bomb blew up part of St. Alphonsus Church on West Broadway. The squad uncovered information that led to the arrest of two Italian anarchists connected with the bombing of St. Patrick's Cathedral and their plan to assassinate John D. Rockefeller, Andrew Carnegie, and J. P. Morgan.

As the Great War progressed in Europe, the Bomb Squad morphed into a covert operation to search for German spies. The squad was well aware of German efforts in the United States to recruit operatives and conduct clandestine activities. The squad had uncovered elements of the Kaiser's fully operational army of United States–based agents. It included a wide range of operatives from academics to longshoremen. Dr. Heinrich Albert, privy counselor and fiscal agent of the German Empire, whose office was in the Hamburg-American Building at 45 Broadway, was spending $2 million to $3 million a week on German propaganda, including having his agents write favorable letters to newspaper editors.

Tunney left for Long Island with a fingerprint expert to determine if Frank Holt was part of a German spy ring and question him about his possession of explosives.

At the courthouse Justice Luyster focused on the allegations against the prisoner. He took statements from Morgan's butler, Physick, the nurse, McCabe, and the two taxi drivers who drove to the Morgan estate.

It was around 4 P.M. when Constable McCahill led the defendant into the crowded courtroom for the official proceedings. The afternoon light poured through the west windows illuminating the man as he walked from the corridor behind to the front of the courtroom in complete view of the spectators. Undoubtedly spectators craned their necks to catch a glimpse of the man who shot J. P. Morgan. The man tottered as he walked in front and stood beside Sheriff Frank McHale and Assistant District Attorney Charles R. Weekes before Judge Luyster. His bandaged head oozed blood. His disheveled clothes hung off his scrawny figure.

The accused was not asked if he wished to have an attorney provided at public expense. It would be another forty-eight years before the United States Supreme Court ruled, in *Gideon v. Wainwright,*[16] that an indigent defendant had the right to appointed counsel at all critical stages in a felony prosecution.

The clerk called for all to rise. Justice Luyster entered the courtroom and took his seat on the bench. The clerk declared the court in session and shouted the name of the case—the only name the clerk had, the one on a card provided to Physick, now in possession of the court. But the better-informed spectators knew that the defendant was not Thomas C. Lester, a representative of the Society Summer Directory.

Justice Luyster asked the defendant for his name.

The defendant had a marked foreign accent. "I am too dignified to discuss the matter."[17]

The defendant was lifting his hand, touching his bandaged head, and muttering in a low groan.

Luyster asked again for his name.

"I have a wife and two children living in Dallas. I am forty years old. I was born in this country and so were my father and mother. A year ago, I became an instructor at Cornell University, in French. I left Ithaca two weeks ago and went to the Mills Hotel in New York at Thirty-Sixth Street and Seventh Avenue."[18]

Interesting, impressive, if true, but still nonresponsive. Justice Luyster's frustration became noticeable. With required restraint, the judge again asked his name.

This time the accused answered, "Frank Holt."[19] There was no other sound except that of the reporters' pencils scratching feverishly on paper.

The judge asked, "Are you a Jew?"[20] Persons speaking with a foreign accent who were carrying dynamite were suspected of nefarious acts. Jews and Italians were recently identified as anarchists.

He replied, "No, I am a Christian gentleman! I am insulted at your remarks. You have no right to assume such an attitude toward a prisoner. I wanted to see Mr. Morgan and to reason with him. I have nothing against him."[21]

The judge could see that the prisoner was playing to the press.

He read the charge: "On the [third] day of July 1915 . . . Frank Holt did commit the crime of assault in the first degree . . . he did willfully, maliciously and feloniously go to the home of J. P. Morgan and with the intent to do bodily harm to the said J. P. Morgan and to kill him."[22]

The defendant suddenly became agitated during the reading and lifted his arm, raised his finger, and pointed at the judge in protest to stop the reading. The officer by his side intervened. The defendant began shouting as loud as he could muster. "Take out all that about the malicious killing! It ought not to be there. There was no malice about it."[23]

The crowd in the back of the courtroom pressed forward to catch every word and a glimpse of the defendant's face.

Sensing that this would be a historic moment in his judicial career, Justice Luyster delivered an admonishment. "I wish you gentlemen in front would all be seated. There are some moving picture men here trying to take pictures."[24] Newsreels had arrived on the scene around 1910.

The judge then directed his attention to Holt. He would not allow this defendant to control the proceedings. "You are charged with assault in the first degree. How do you wish to plead?"[25]

Holt responded, "I don't know what you mean. But I do want to object to the part that tells about malicious killing. You seem to think that my sympathies are pro-German. That is not the case. I am merely against wholesale slaughter."[26]

When the judge told him his shots wounded Mr. Morgan, he responded, "I did not hurt him, I shot to frighten him. I hope he isn't hurt. I shot away from him just so that he might be frightened. You can do as you wish with me. I did my duty, you do yours."[27]

The judge asked if he had any accomplices.

"No one was in this but me and God Almighty. I had no other accomplices."[28]

Looking bedraggled, with his collar missing, shirt speckled with blood, jacket torn and trousers in sorry condition, he swayed back and forth as if about to pass out. He threw his arm out and became unstable. He was supported by the officer. Another deputy sprang forward and caught him on the other side.

The judge patiently explained that the charges carried a penalty of up to ten years imprisonment.

He asked, "How do you wish to proceed?" He stared at the perpetrator for a moment and without any response spoke slowly, "Do you desire a preliminary examination now?"[29]

The defendant ignored the judge and turned his head toward the crowd of spectators, more interested in the crowd and reporters than his own fate.

A defendant who has been arrested without a warrant has a right to a preliminary hearing on whether there was probable cause for his arrest. But there was no request for a hearing, only a demand to modify the charge. The request was denied. The defendant refused to enter a plea of guilty or not guilty to the charge. He once again seemed to control the proceedings and the narrative.

Apparently unwilling to allow any more showmanship by the prisoner, Justice Luyster found that Holt was not competent to enter his own plea and entered a plea of "not guilty" on his behalf.

Assistant District Attorney Weekes suggested that all further proceedings be postponed until Wednesday, July 7, at ten o'clock, when Holt would appear for a formal arraignment in New York State Supreme Court, the trial court for felonies in the county seat of Mineola.

The judge granted the postponement and adjourned the proceeding. The defendant was held without bail and returned to his cell.

The newsmen Judge Luyster accommodated during the proceedings were anxious to broadcast the biggest story to the country and the world. The Associated Press service, a cooperative news venture, provided telegraphic reports to member newspapers.

Reporters far from Glen Cove were knocking on the door at Cornell University administrators and faculty asking about their language instructor and PhD conferee who was now accused of the assassination attempt on J. P. Morgan.

The Cornell community was measured in its response with the preservation of reputation foremost in mind.

Frank Holt was identified as a faculty member for the past two years. The university tasked the German Department with creating and issuing an appropriate statement to the press. The artfully crafted statement said that if Frank Holt committed the crimes of which he was accused, he must have been mentally unbalanced. His acts were totally inconsistent with those of the person they knew. He was known to sympathize with Germany in the war but was always regarded as a most reasonable man. The only indiscretion that Faust, the chairman of the department, would mention was Frank leaving Cornell without submitting final grades. Other members of the Cornell German Department described their colleague as leading a "blameless life," having an ideal family life and being a devoted husband and a wonderful father. He was a conscientious, hard-working teacher and student, a reserved, reticent type but with good habits. The *Ithaca Journal* Saturday evening paper ran the headline story of the attempted assassination of Morgan and the Cornell professor who was charged.

In Texas, the *Fort Worth Star-Telegram* banner headline read "Crank Shoots J. P. Morgan." The newspaper identified the assailant as F. Holt, "an instructor in French at Cornell University."[30] This same newspaper announced in April that Frank Holt of Cornell University had been appointed as chairman of the language department of Southern Methodist University. Word spread quickly that Reverend Sensabaugh's daughter, Leona, was married to the would-be assassin. There was little peace inside the Sensabaugh home. A continuous stream of church members and neighbors visited out of sympathy or perhaps curiosity.

Reverend Sensabaugh sent a telegram to Frank requesting information at the only location he had represented he was staying—the Mills Hotel. The wording of his telegram indicated the family's disbelief of the events that had occurred at the Morgan mansion and their skepticism that the esteemed scholar, husband, and son-in-law could possibly be the perpetrator.

Reporters were at the door of the reverend with questions. Sensabaugh told the press that Frank and Leona were married for ten years. In reality, it had only been five years. He ended the statement by saying, "Frank has not answered any of my telegrams."[31]

Journalists were not content with the reverend's initial statement. With continuous clamoring from the press for a further statement, Reverend Sensabaugh realized he had few choices but to prepare a slightly more fulsomely worded communiqué: "If I do learn that it was my son-in-law who shot Mr. Morgan, I will make a statement to the public. Until then, I can say nothing. He has been a perfect gentleman in the ten years he has been married to my daughter and if he really did such a thing, there can be only one reason. He must be. . . ."[32]

He stopped reading as if the words that had been written were not what he wanted to say. A sympathetic reporter shouted, "It must be mental aberration!"[33]

And the reverend agreed, "it could be nothing else."[34]

The press was denied direct access to Leona. Leona was tight-lipped, even to family members, about the letters and telegrams she received from her husband. Her father, perhaps laying the groundwork to explain away incriminating statements, speculated that Holt's correspondence to his daughter "might be the work of someone else."[35]

The reverend, now in the national spotlight, showed few traces of emotion as he talked with reporters. He faced his interviewers as calmly as if he were speaking to his congregation, until the reporters repeatedly asked for a comment on the criminal actions of "your son-in-law." Each time, his voice dropped an octave when he corrected the statement by saying, "*If* it *is* my son-in-law."[36]

Later in the day, the reverend received confirmation that his son-in-law was the Morgan shooter. The reporters were back wanting more. Why would his son-in-law shoot Morgan? Was he part of a German spy ring? Is he an anarchist? The reverend, who had not seen Frank in more than four years, prepared another statement. This response seemed to originate with Leona. Frank's life was above reproach and consistent with Secretary of State Bryan's peace plans. Bryan had resigned from office a month earlier protesting President Wilson's condemnation of the sinking of the *Lusitania* in which Wilson did not acknowledge what he possibly knew were munitions onboard.

Soon the reverend shifted his responses to the press from outright denial to declaration that "temporary insanity must have caused the deed."[37] The reverend told reporters that Frank was of German descent, and he had been closely associated with the German professors at Cornell, portraying his son-in-law in a most positive light. "Naturally, his sympathies were with Germany, but above all, he desired peace. Frank was like Tolstoy in his belief in non-resistance."[38] But somewhere in the back of his mind, the reverend knew that six years before, his fellow board members at Polytechnic College denied Frank a faculty position because his background could not be verified.

The reverend's statements made headline news across the country.

When the news about the attempt on Morgan's life hit the Washington, DC, papers, many residents were still shaken by the sound and vibrations of the explosion that occurred at midnight. The fear of the unknown was unsettling.

Four detectives were assigned to find the bomber. There was a report of a suspicious man "resembling a Spaniard"[39] passing through the Capitol grounds on Friday night. Detectives found the suspect, but he was not near the Capitol on Thursday or Friday. There were no leads other than on page two of the Saturday edition of the *Evening Star*, where the paper quoted from a strange letter it had received from a R. A. Pearce. "Unusual times and circumstances call for unusual means. WE stand for PEACE AND GOOD WILL to all men. A prostitute sells out for a dollar FI! Columbia too?"[40]

Pearce compared American bankers to "prostitutes" in their voracious appetite for wealth regardless of the cost to human life. He accused businesses of "getting rich" from "blood money," and called on "real Americans" to stop the "wholesale murder." Pearce took responsibility for the bombing of the Capitol. The irony of using explosives as a means to end the selling of explosives was not lost on the writer: "Sorry I had to use explosives. (Never again.) This explosion is the exclamation point to my appeal for Peace! R. Pearce."[41]

At the Washington, DC, Police Department, Assistant Superintendent Boardman was conducting his investigation of the Capitol bombing. Boardman read over and over the letter to the newspapers signed "R. Pearce," who claimed he was the bomber.

Boardman could not brush aside the nation's biggest story—the Morgan shooting and the dynamite found in the Long Island assailant's possession. The newspapers set out the statements made by the would-be assassin Frank Holt to Judge Luyster. After Boardman read the statement, it crystalized before him:

R. A. Pearce	*Frank Holt*
We would, of course not sell to the Germans if they could buy here, and since so far we only sold to the Allies, neither side should object if we stopped.[42]	If Germany should be able to buy munitions here we would, of course positively refuse to sell to her.[43]

Boardman immediately wired his superior Major Pullman, who happened to be visiting New York: "Ascertain from F. Holt, in custody at Glen Cove, NY, for shooting J. P. Morgan, his whereabouts Thursday and Friday, as he may have placed the bomb in the Capitol here Friday night."[44]

As it later turned out, Major Pullman had been on the same train and in the next car as Frank traveled from DC to New York on the midnight train arriving on the morning of July 3.

The public's curiosity was unbounded about the Cornell PhD-turned-assassin and whether J. P. Morgan would survive. Matinicock became an armed camp. No one would have free access to East Island. Sheriff Pettit sent a detail of twelve county detectives and several police officers with shotguns and revolvers. Charles Price, the groundskeeper, now carried a repeating rifle and stood watch at the gatehouse on the bridge. He, like the other Morgan employees, was determined to protect his employer and family. When a reporter asked to enter, he said, "I wouldn't let you enter even if it were not against orders for they might take a pot shot at you. There are a score of men with shotguns up there on the grounds."[45]

The newlyweds, Mr. and Mrs. Junius Spencer Morgan, arrived at Matinicock in the afternoon for the party in their honor. They suspected serious trouble upon seeing the guard at the entrance to East Island.

They asked questions and put the guard in an awkward position. The couple had obviously not heard the news. The guard told Junius his father had been "injured." Junius rushed to the main house and then up the stairs to his parents' bedroom. His father was in bed attended by two physicians and three trained nurses from the City. Junius was anxious to speak with the doctors and find out the details of his father's condition.

The New York City doctors finally arrived at the Morgan estate, and at 3:30 P.M. issued an unnarrated statement: "An examination of Mr. Morgan discloses that there are two bullet wounds in the region of the right hip. There are no unfavorable symptoms and he is resting easily. H. M. Lyle, J. W. Marcoe."[46]

Everyone seemed to be in a state of disbelief and unable to relay clearly the events of the day. His grandmother, Pierpont's widow, Frances, had arrived and was distressed. Junius's aunts Louisa and Juliet tried to calm their anguished mother. The mansion was filled with family in a concerned and solemn state.

Other family members and friends arrived to attend a party and were asked to leave after they were told of the attempt on Jack's life and his injuries.

Junius finally spoke with Physick and the household help who were witnesses to the assassination attempt.

After getting another update from the doctors, Junius spoke to the press. At 6:15 P.M., Junius read a prepared statement stating that the bullets did not hit any vital organs.

The reporters asked, "Is your father able to walk around?"[47]

Junius answered, "No, he has been confined to his bed."[48]

Heavy on everyone's mind was the recent memory of President McKinley, who was shot twice in the abdomen and appeared to improve in the days that followed, only to die seven days later.

Although intruders had burglarized the Morgan home three times, Jack had escaped any assault and had refused to assist in the prosecution of the perpetrators. Some of the locals said he was too kindhearted. A crew member on board the *Corsair* remembered his genteel nature: "And do you know, if Morgan was a few minutes late, he'd apologize to the crew for keeping them waiting. He was a good man no matter how many millions of dollars he had."[49]

At the Glen Cove courthouse the defendant was asked if he wanted to prepare a written statement before he was transported to Mineola. He indicated that he did and requested that his statement be distributed to the newspapers, eager to sway public opinion to his noble mission: "My motive in coming was to try to force Mr. Morgan to use his influence with the manufacturers of munitions in the United States and with the millionaires who are financing the war loans to have an embargo put on the shipments of war munitions. . . . and would it not be better for us to make what money we can without causing the slaughter of Europeans."[50]

Reporters were permitted to speak with the defendant in his cell. But it was the *Brooklyn Daily Eagle* reporter who had been present in the courtroom and now got the scoop, an interview with the prisoner. He described the defendant as "having been beaten and battered to a state of semi-consciousness by the Morgan servants after he had shot their master. He complained that his head ached fearfully and seemed dazed, but his speech was calm and delivered in that quiet, almost effeminate tone which is the peculiarity of so many persons of unsound mind who may be classified as dangerous."[51]

The reporter then vaulted question after question at the prisoner. He responded with a distinct German accent and reassured his listener, sounding somewhat condescending, that "I have a well-trained mind and I studied for a long time as to what would be the proper course for me to pursue before I decided to take the matter up with Mr. Morgan personally."[52]

The prisoner, addressing the *Brooklyn Eagle*'s reporter in a patronizing tone, said, "Now, really, young man, if you but stop and think clearly, you must surely realize I would not come here on the mission I did and then kill Mr. Morgan even before I had spoken to him?"[53]

"But why did you come armed with revolvers and dynamite?"[54]

"Well, I did not know what might happen, coming on the mission. I did and to such a place as I did, I had to be prepared."[55]

"Why did you carry a bottle of nitroglycerin? To what use did you expect to put that?"[56]

"Nitroglycerin? Oh some fool upstairs called that nitroglycerin. It was really alcohol, or benzine, or something like that just for removing spots from my clothing you know."[57]

"How did Mr. Morgan act? How did he receive you?"[58]

"Very, very courageously. I admire his courage very greatly. It was superb, exactly as I should have expected."[59] And sarcastically he added, "If he would use that courage in the proper direction I am sure he will get somewhere in this world."[60]

The shooter undoubtedly sought to portray himself as gallant and gentlemanly in heaping praise on the courage of the man he shot. But with the press eating out of his hand, he could not resist the snide insinuation that Morgan had yet to accomplish anything in life.

"And Mrs. Morgan?"[61]

"She also was courageous. But at last, she became just a woman. She was just screaming about and making very much noise."[62]

He then told the reporter that he would refuse to answer any questions if he was asked a second time if he or any member of his family was a "subject of Germany."[63]

"Mr. Morgan did not give me a fair chance to say anything to him. He jumped at me and grappled with me. There was a lot of screaming and I fired in the air. I admire Mr. Morgan's courage."[64]

Then he asked the reporter, "Have you a bit of paper?"[65]

The reporter obliged.

"Thank you so much. And a pencil if you don't mind."[66]

Then he wrote a telegram:

> Mrs. Frank Holt, No. 101 South Marseilles Street, Dallas, Texas:
> *Man proposes. God disposes. Don't come here until you get my letters. Be strong. FRANK.*[67]

The phrase Frank used is from book I, chapter 19, of *The Imitation of Christ,* a fifteenth-century book by the German cleric Thomas à Kempis.

He called the guard and handed him the statement. As to the required postage he said, "You have money upstairs to pay for it. You know you took my cash from me when you brought me here."[68]

It was late afternoon when Captain Tunney arrived at the small Glen Cove courthouse to interrogate the prisoner. He asked the officer in charge for Frank to be brought out of his cell for questioning. In the narrow ten-foot corridor of the dark basement, Tunney and Frank sat on camp stools. Tunney described Frank as a "frail, slight fellow, with deep eye sockets, a prominent hook nose and a retreating chin."[69] There was no doubt this prisoner spoke with a German accent. Frank provided some background information about his parents who were foreign born, his wife and children in Dallas, and his teaching history. He spoke only of having stayed at the Mills Hotel in the last few weeks.

Tunney asked, "What did you try to kill Mr. Morgan for?"[70]

"I didn't intend to kill him. I wanted to persuade him to use his influence to stop the shipment of ammunition to Europe."[71]

"Well, you chose a pretty strong means of persuading him, didn't you? What was the dynamite for?"[72]

"I was going to show him what was causing all the trouble—explosives."[73]

When asked about why he had written the Morgan children's names on the piece of paper found in his pocket, he described his plan to hold them as hostages in exchange for Morgan's promise to stop funding the Allies. Tunney tried to pry out of Holt where he purchased the dynamite but instead he received the addresses of the Hoboken pawn shops where he purchased the revolvers. Tunney passed along the pawn shop information to headquarters.

The interrogation ended because the county police cars had come to take the prisoner to the Nassau County jail in Mineola. Before being whisked away, the photographers lingered to capture a picture of Constable McCahill and Deputy Sheriff Theodore Campbell outside the courthouse with a bandaged Frank Holt standing erect.

Justice Luyster accompanied McCahill in a county automobile. He did not want to miss the opportunity to escort the notorious suspect to the county jail since his entire career had been spent in local Nassau County politics and for the first time, he was the man of significance.

Upon arrival at the county jail, detectives took their turn at questioning the prisoner.

"Do you think you are crazy?"[74]

"I don't know. Sometimes I do; sometimes I don't. I've been trying for six months to convince myself of one of two things, either that I am crazy or that I am not. And I haven't been able to settle the question yet."[75] Was the intelligent scholar toying with the county detectives?

Captain Tunney, whose jurisdiction did not extend to Nassau County, muscled his way into a lead role in the investigation. Holt's admission that he spent time at the Mills Hotel in Manhattan was a slender reed on which to base the primacy of the New York City Police Department. But it was undeniable that Holt had access to dynamite, and the danger to ships in the New York harbor was of great national concern, and Tunney was the captain of the Bomb Squad.

Frank had been battered in the takedown at the Morgan home and his head throbbed. He had been harried with questions and was exhausted.

To Tunney, these were the perfect conditions for Frank to break down and disclose information. But the man who had concealed his identity for the past nine years was not so easily broken.

Tunney ordered the guards to take the prisoner out into the corridor with a man on each side to support him and walk him up and down until his stumbling feet dragged listlessly over the cement floor. Then they sat him down for more questioning. Tunney continued to interrogate. At times, Holt's answers were barely audible and other times, he refused to answer. He was pulled back up on to his feet and dragged through the corridors.

Tunney suggested that they go for a ride to where he had been the day before. A mob of reporters waited outside the jail like vultures ready to pounce on their prey. Holt protested and accused Tunney of wanting "to make a show of me to the morbid crowd."[76]

The papers reported that Tunney used unorthodox methods of "sweating" the prisoner. The "Third Degree" was an interrogation technique used by the NYPD to squeeze information from unrelenting prisoners. It was a play on the name of New York's top detective in the nineteenth century, Thomas F. Byrnes, who was known as "Third Degree Byrnes."

Tunney questioned him step by step about the Capitol bombing. Frank's words revealed nothing new. Tunney's goal was to cajole him into revealing the identity of possible confederates, but Frank wasn't budging: "I have not talked to my friends about it. . . . Do you suppose that a university professor would undertake that sort of thing?"[77]

Tunney was frustrated.

Tunney decided to shift gears and conduct a more formal interview at the jailhouse with a detective from the county, two sheriffs, and a stenographer. Tunney's simple question of the location of Holt's birth garnered a response of "Somehow my brain is in such shape that I can't remember—Wisconsin, I know."[78]

Tunny would press, "You speak with a German accent. Were you born in Germany?"[79]

"Now listen, this has been said before that I speak with a foreign accent. That is because I speak several languages . . . French, German, Spanish."[80]

"How many times have you been to Philadelphia?"

"No time."

"You have a clipping of a Philadelphia newspaper."

"I saw that lying around somewhere."

"Where did you sleep last night?"[81]

"Now I will tell you. A reporter from the Associated Press asked me about this Washington business, and he was trying to connect me with that. I suppose that is what you are trying to do."[82]

"I am not trying to connect you with anything. I want truthful answers. I am very frank and honest with you. I will fairly investigate every answer that you make."[83]

"I wasn't in Washington Friday at all. I was in New York. I had my breakfast and lunch downtown at the Mills Hotel at Thirty-Sixth Street and Seventh Avenue. So you see, I couldn't have been in Washington."[84]

And then Frank assessed the situation and abruptly changed course. Whatever his motive was, it did not include contrition. "I wrote that R. Pearce letter. I was in Washington yesterday and came back on the train."[85]

As far as Tunney was concerned, this statement was tantamount to a confession by Frank Holt that he was the Capitol bomber.

The county detective slipped out the door and sent a telegram to Washington. Assistant Superintendent Boardman: "Frank Holt placed dynamite bomb in Capitol building at 4 P.M. yesterday. Left Washington on midnight train to New York."[86]

Holt continued to speak and purported to disclose his method of bomb-making. He created the bomb by gouging out sticks of dynamite, then combined the contents with trick match heads and a bottle of sulfuric acid. Tunney, an expert on explosives, doubted the defendant's methodology. When asked to expand on his unusual bomb-making technique, Holt gave a cryptic response:

"Well, you see, I had experimented on it before."[87]

The improbability of this scholar of linguistics becoming an expert in bomb-making was later the subject of much debate. He said he waited until a time when there would be few tourists who might see him.

At 7:00 P.M. Assistant Superintendent Boardman was handed the telegraph reporting Holt's confession to the bombing of the Capitol. The Washington investigation would continue to determine if Frank acted alone or with others.

Major Pullman of the District of Columbia police arrived at the Mineola jail and asked Frank, "Why did you decide to go to the Capitol?[88]

"Merely to get the most prominent place in the country. You see I wanted to call attention to my appeal."[89]

Every statement made by the prisoner was leaked to the eager press, then fed to teletype machines, which tapped out the news from wire services and was printed in the next day's papers across the country. It seemed as if everyone in the nation was waiting for more answers.

Tunney strongly suspected that there was more dynamite and a broader, more sophisticated plot. He analyzed every piece of evidence. Frank's finances caught Tunney's eye. He established that the prisoner spent $275 in the last two weeks, excluding the cost of the dynamite. There was $40 found in Frank's pocket. Tunney uncovered the bank withdrawals Frank made before leaving Ithaca, one for $600 and another a week later for $500. The amount of cash didn't add up. Frank's yearly income from Cornell and tutoring totaled $1,500. Tunney calculated that since January, Frank had received $750 and paid for ordinary expenses for a family of four. A bank balance of $1,100 was impossible without funding from an outside source. Tunny's conviction grew stronger that there was more dynamite stashed somewhere, and Frank's actions were not those of a lone wolf.

Frank denied ever visiting well-known places that German spies or operatives frequented such as the German Club, Pabst's in Columbus Circle, and Luchow's Restaurant. He was still unable to provide a city of his birth.

He repeatedly said he fired his weapon only to frighten Morgan, and the financier was wounded only because he became violent and threw himself at him instead of waiting to listen to him.

While Tunney was interrogating the defendant, McCahill brought in Holt's property from Glen Cove. He and others had previously searched the prisoner's suitcase and presumably it no longer contained explosives. McCahill had cataloged the items at the Glen Cove courthouse, but he was surprised to find a concealed pocket in the suitcase, and hidden between two thin sheets of leather was a typewritten letter to His Majesty the Kaiser, written in German.

> My Dear Sir:
> Let me assure you that I represent the ideal American. My name is either known to you or will be in a day or two, so don't brush this letter aside as of no importance.[90]

He wrote a protracted recommendation to the Kaiser for the best way for Germany to win American support—desist Germany's "land grabbing," which placed it in an unfavorable light. He believed the war was a result of "the natural growth of the nations and of commercial rivalry, which is perfectly legitimate and healthy." He recommended "applying their private Christianity to public affairs, [which were] bound by a long tradition of lying diplomacy."[91]

That evening, 214 miles from Mineola, in the small offices of the Chief of Police for the City of Cambridge, Massachusetts, Inspector Patrick Hurley sat at his desk reading the local evening newspapers. Banner headlines announced the shooting of the famous financier. Hurley was mesmerized by the description of the perpetrator—a Cornell instructor with a slim build and an awkward gait. He reread the defendant's identifying characteristics. He had a flashback from nine years before when he had received a call from the Cambridge medical examiner, Dr. Swan, about a suspicious death of a young mother. Her husband was a Harvard instructor who disappeared. One distinct physical feature of the fugitive was that he was a "loose jointed walker," and this was noted in the information circulated by the Cambridge police to other police departments around the country. Hurley's yearly caseload was heavy, and nine years was a long time to remember any one miscreant, but murder-by-poisoning by a Harvard professor was a rare occurrence in the city of Cambridge and it was the distinctive feature of this alleged assassin, his "shambling walk," that caused Hurley to ruminate. Could this assassin be the wife murderer too? He wasted no time and sent Muenter's record to New York.

CHAPTER 24

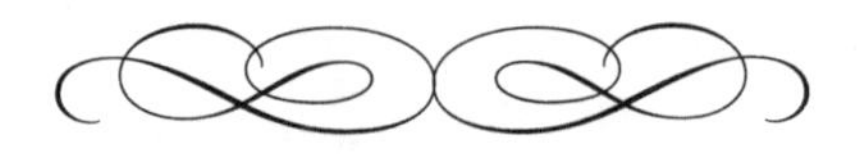

July 4

Dynamite

On the morning of July 4, Tunney's Bomb Squad tracked down two Pennsylvania Railroad employees on the Washington to New York overnight run who remembered a man that fit the description of Frank Holt on the train. J. L. Riland, the conductor, and James N. Purcell, the head brakeman, recalled that the train left DC on the night of July 2 and arrived in New York on July 3 at 5:56 A.M. Riland identified Frank and said, he sat "in the 'cubby-hole' by the washstand in the smoking car. Holt occupied lower berth number six in car twenty-seven." He did not smoke and selected a seat so that he was riding backward, which was odd when there were so many seats facing forward. "He sat by himself and appeared to be half asleep."[1]

Tunney spent Independence Day morning trying to eke more information from Frank in the Nassau County jail. He was haunted by the possibility there was additional dynamite somewhere. It was critical to find out where and why Frank bought the dynamite. Now Holt had a new refrain. He would tell all on Wednesday, July 7. Why Wednesday? What would happen then? Holt had been selective in his disclosures, saying nothing about confederates or the source and location of dynamite. Now he was taunting Tunney with his pledge to tell all in three days, but not a moment sooner.

He refused to eat or drink. A guard was ordered to move the defendant to a larger cell on the first floor, where he was watched continuously.

Dr. Guy Cleghorn, the jail physician, examined Holt and reported no notable concerns.

While sitting in the cell, he asked the guard for paper and pencil. He wrote to his wife:

> My Dear—
> I just want to say that I am well taken care of. Kiss my babies for me and let U. S. all bear this burden with dignity and faith in the all-loving father who will yet lead us aright.
> Affectionately,
> Frank[2]

He responded to his father-in-law's request for "particulars" about the allegations but was perplexed as to why he was asking for information when he had previously kept Leona apprised. Out of respect for his father-in-law, he suggested he look at his previous letters and asked him not to come to Mineola. "I am well taken care of, and the grand jury cannot meet until September. I am held without bail plea without guilty. So I just wait, though I wish that death might come to end it all at once. Life under these conditions is unspeakably horrible."[3]

He provided his father-in-law with a revised rendition of the event at the Morgan House and how he "did right." Now his story included the two Morgan children, who he claimed were in the parlor, and willingly followed him upstairs. He said his mistake was to walk in front of the children instead of behind them. At the top of the stairs, he met with a screaming Mr. and Mrs. Morgan, who attacked him. "This physical courage overruled my moral courage."[4] They rolled on the floor and he tried to shoot in the air, but someone grabbed his hand, which caused Mr. Morgan to get "hurt." Then he repeated his refrain about the war and the slaughter that must stop and an embargo on arms, ending his letter with: "God bless us all. I am in His hand, so don't worry about me. With much love, Affly. FRANK."[5]

Holt's letters were leaked and his words reported. His vision for peace did not improve his public reputation as a bomber and would-be assassin. But his reputation would soon get worse.

•

In Dallas, the Sensabaughs could not hide from the story that was gripping the nation. Frank's graduation photo from the Polytechnic College covered the front page of the *Dallas Daily Times Herald* with the caption, "The Man Who Shot J. P. Morgan and Tried to Dynamite the Capitol."[6]

When a reporter asked the reverend about Frank's apparent confession to bombing the Capitol, he responded, "Oh, that can't be true, but I thank you for telling me. I begged him not to go to New York this summer. He has just overworked himself."[7] When asked about Frank's German accent, the reverend remembered only a lisp, no accent, repeated that his life was exemplary.

The family stuck to the same script. Frank wanted peace, his life was above reproach, and his views aligned with those of the former Secretary of State Bryan, who espoused neutrality.

The press reported that Leona was in terrible shock from the "catastrophe." She would not remain silent while her husband's reputation was sullied in the press. It was time for her to come forward and repair her husband's honor and restore the Sensabaugh family's good name. She granted the *Dallas Daily Times Herald* an "exclusive" interview, which turned out to be nothing more than a prepared statement delivered by "Judge" Joseph E. Cockrell, the family friend and confidante: "She had no suspicion of any 'mental trouble' and that a 'little rest' would not help and certainly there was no evidence of ill will against Mr. Morgan. I am hoping against hope that there has been some frightful mistake. I was in constant communication with him by letters and there was nothing to indicate any such outbreak."[8]

Cockrell provided the press with parts of a letter from Frank, dated July 3, postmarked from New York, mailed before he took the train to Glen Cove. In the letter, Frank tells Leona he had been sick, despondent, and continued to work in Manhattan on his research for his upcoming faculty appointment at SMU. Leona, via Cockrell, presented a litany of reasons for Frank's behavior—stress from overwork, a nervous breakdown, and a recent diagnosis of "tuberculosis of the bones,"[9] which caused severe headaches, weight loss, and insomnia.

In 1891, the *Medical News* published an article on tuberculosis of the bones and joints and referenced a treatment involving the resection of the hip. Could this have been the reason for his disjointed walk?

Cockrell alluded in passing to the Capitol bombing and Morgan shooting as a "misfortune." He said Leona wanted to highlight her husband's stellar academic achievements and offered to get the Cornell faculty to confirm it, if necessary. Then, in some bizarre effort to help her husband, Leona released a poem Frank wrote to her while they were in college:

When I am dead
Will friends look long upon my face,
Then pallid, still and cold in death.
And speak of honest worth and faith
Beloved, flowers now you cast
No fragrance lend to hours past;
Belated words of love and tears
Will never ease the broken years.
Frank[10]

Leona found time to write a letter to the storage company in Ithaca, requesting that her property and furniture be cared for until she was able to retrieve it.

There was more shocking news coming to the Sensabaugh family.

•

Reporters continued to hound any Cornell faculty members remaining in Ithaca in July for usable quotes. The burning question of the moment was whether Holt was actually Erich Muenter. No one was willing to confirm his dual identity or go on record with an unkind word. Cornell Prof. A. W. Boesche, of the German Department, told a reporter only that he wished to express his sympathy for the plight of this instructor, who was in an unfortunate predicament.

A maid was assigned to clean the quarters in Sage Cottage on the Cornell campus where Frank lived after Leona left for Texas. She found an unmarked trunk. When she opened it, it was packed with letters in German and English addressed to Frank Holt, and hundreds of newspaper clippings. She immediately called the Ithaca police. The trunk was sent to Tunney's Bomb Squad in Manhattan. This gave investigators hope they could unmask Holt's true identity and those of his contacts and confederates. It might also have clues to future plans for destruction and mayhem.

The more than two hundred letters described Holt's interest in mining ventures in Mexico and a real-estate scheme in Florida. A few letters from 1910 and 1911 revealed that Frank owed considerable amounts of money. There were letters written in German and stacks of news clippings of stories not typically of interest to an academic. The trunk revealed a very different person from the one portrayed by his wife, father-in-law, and colleagues.

Some of the clipped headline stories found in the trunk were bizarre and macabre: "Chicago Lunatic at Large" and "Rape Case of Insane," discussing an incident at the Kankakee, Illinois, asylum; "Suffers for Brother's Crime,"[11] about a murderer in Manitowoc, Wisconsin, sentenced to life in prison and going insane; details of the brutal stabbing murder of Mabel Page by Charles L. Tucker in Massachusetts and his subsequent trial and execution; and an account of a wife who murdered her husband and hid his body in a container. Frank closely followed the murder of Stanford White and the trials of his accused deranged murderer Harry Thaw. There was an editorial from the *Chicago Tribune* titled "The Danger of Overstudy,"[12] which was about a college professor who had gone insane by spending long hours studying criminology and warned against arduous and prolonged mental work.

The trunk held a dozen articles reporting "Negro" lynchings. The Bomb Squad's attention was quickly drawn to those articles about the calculated, premeditated murder of a young mother after childbirth by her husband, a Harvard professor who had administered arsenic in lethal doses. The professor was said to be an expert in the lore of witchcraft. In an article describing Erich Muenter, Frank underlined the word "brilliant."[13]

Among the letters there were two photographs, one of his wife and the other of an unidentified little girl. Could this have been his daughter, Helen, whom he abandoned?

One newspaper described the trunk contents as a "literary chamber of horrors in the form of clippings on murder and insanity."[14]

Hidden among the papers was a .38 caliber revolver.

•

At Matinicock, Jack continued to rest. He'd slept all afternoon the day of the attack. An X-ray confirmed that he'd suffered no broken bones. The area surrounding the Morgan estate was closely watched, including the arrival of passengers at the Glen Cove station. Jack's sister and brother-in-law, Louisa and Herbert Satterlee, prayed at the Union

Chapel in Lattingtown. Prayers for Jack were offered at all Glen Cove houses of worship.

Out of respect, the New York Yacht Club, where Jack was vice commodore, postponed its July 4 race. When Jack learned of the rescheduling, he objected and refused to "hear of having the trial [race] called off on his account."[15] He was part owner of the sloop *Resolute,* slated to participate in the race.

•

With Frank Holt's photograph stamped on the first page of newspapers across the country, Theodore W. Hiller, who had rented the Cambridge apartment at 107 Oxford Street to the Muenter family, stared at the picture and in a moment of gestalt, declared that this man was indeed Erich Muenter. He informed the authorities.

The local reporters caught the story and canvassed the neighborhood. Another Cambridge neighbor told a reporter, "There is a remarkably striking resemblance between this man and Muenter."[16]

Dr. McIntyre, who attempted to treat Leone Muenter before and after childbirth, was now questioned about the identity of Frank Holt. He was not interested in getting further embroiled in the crimes of Erich Muenter. Nine years before, he had been required to testify before Judge Almy and the grand jury. He looked at the photo and would only agree that it bore a strong resemblance to Erich but would not commit to a firm identification.

•

The *Chicago Tribune* reported that Cambridge police believed that Frank Holt and Erich Muenter were the same man. The paper featured side-by-side photographs of Frank and Erich.

An anonymous source confirmed to the *Chicago Tribune* that the Morgan shooter was Erich Muenter, who fled after his wife's death and was a fugitive from the law. Reporters were once again back on the beat. They tracked down Erich Muenter's sister Bertha, in Chicago, and asked her if she believed Frank Holt was her brother Erich. She said that was impossible. She had not heard from her brother since his disappearance in 1906.

CHAPTER 25

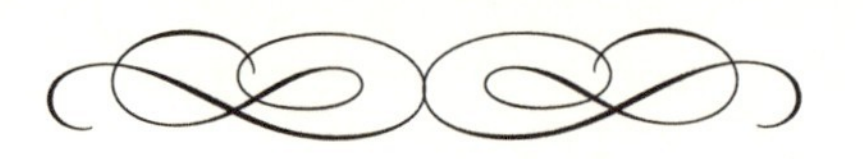

July 5

Erich Muenter

Tunney went back to the jailhouse determined to get some information from Frank but to no avail. Frank would repeat his mantra: he would tell all on Wednesday, July 7.

Tunney needed to find the stash of dynamite and retraced the prisoner's every step. His multiple aliases had sent Tunney on a wild goose chase with a receipt from a storage area in the Pennsylvania train station. Tunney was familiar with the methods of German spy rings and their use of aliases, and he needed to figure out what alias Holt had used to purchase the dynamite for its storage. He asked Frank why a purportedly sincere antiwar activist needed to use aliases. Frank's flippant response was that it popped into his head.

The prisoner was refusing to ingest any food or liquids. He spent a restless night and morning, tossing about his cot, continuously muttering to himself. His cries became louder, and he began pacing the floor of his cell, waving his arms and shouting over and over again, "O God, I want to die! Show me a way to die!"[1] He said he had failed to stop war supplies to German enemies and was a disgrace to his family and friends in Texas.

Leona sent him a telegram with a loving message in an effort to sooth and comfort him.

> Everything is all right. It is your duty now to rest and let your (loved) ones and God take care of you. All your friends send love. If you can let us know

when you get this, do so.
Mrs. FRANK HOLT[2]

Frank called the guard and asked for a pencil and paper to write back to his wife. The guards recognized that this prisoner was no common criminal. Down-on-their luck inmates rarely asked to write anyone. Frank was articulate and well educated. They read about his stature in the academic community, his wife and children. Frank responded to Leona's telegram,

> I am through with life. I don't care to live anymore. I hope you will bring up the little ones to be God-fearing men and women.
> FRANK[3]

Five minutes later, a guard passed by the prisoner's cell and saw him writhing in pain. Blood was flowing from his wrist. The flesh had a jagged cut. The prisoner had ripped the eraser from the pencil's ferrule and used the metal band to slash an artery in his left wrist. The guard was stunned and angry that he had been duped into giving him a pencil.

The guard yelled for help and seconds later, backup came. The pencil was found on the cot. Warden Hult ordered that Frank's belt and suspenders be removed.

Dr. Cleghorn was summoned. The cut bled incessantly but no ligaments or tendons were torn. The doctor bandaged the wound. He observed Frank retching. The prisoner had taken to rambling when he spoke and repeated that his duty was "now complete" and appeared satisfied that he "acted with full approval of God."[4] Cleghorn opined that the defendant suffered from paranoia and/or dementia praecox. Dr. Cleghorn was aware of the advanced theories of psychiatry by a German psychiatrist, Dr. Emil Kraepelin. Kraepelin's study, published in 1899, described paranoia as a personality disorder with delusional aspects. Dementia praecox, according to Kraepelin, was a biological illness, today known as schizophrenia. Cleghorn reported to the press that Holt was "unsound when he attacked Mr. Morgan and he is unsound now. The only place for the man is the Matteawan asylum."[5]

Matteawan State Hospital for the Criminally Insane was established in 1892. Recent history had shown that confinement to Matteawan was a viable temporary option, preferable to incarceration for the mentally ill. Its celebrity inmate, Harry Kendall Thaw, a wealthy heir of a coal and railroad magnate, murdered Stanford White before hundreds of people on the rooftop of Madison Square Garden. He was found not guilty by reason of insanity. He was sent to Matteawan and began a six-year process of petitioning for release, claiming he was no longer insane.

Frank Holt held a high opinion of himself and undoubtedly considered himself more resourceful and clever than Thaw.

The warden ordered additional security for a suicide watch. Jeremiah Ryan, a special deputy sheriff, was added to the detail for the sole and exclusive purpose of watching Holt during the night shift.

Tunney returned to the jail with the district attorney of Nassau County, Lewis J. Smith. Smith had been contacted by Ott, the landlord from Central Park, who recognized Holt's picture in the newspaper.

Ott told Smith that Holt said his name was "Totten." "He came to me in Central Park two weeks ago, Thursday. He has not been around here since last Friday when he went away with a trunk. There's a lot of stuff around the place now that you may want."[6]

Smith relayed the information to Tunney. Now Tunney's head was racing with theories and possible connections. This subdued college instructor had navigated areas no academic would travel using deception and subterfuge. Tunney would later write when he became aware of another alias: "This Pearce-Lester-Holt-Henderson-Muenter was becoming more interesting every minute. Wife-poisoner, dynamiter, gunman—what next?"[7]

The question of his identity continued to puzzle the authorities. By happenstance, Assistant District Attorney Charles R. Wood of Nassau County was a student at Harvard at the same time Erich Muenter was an instructor and PhD student. They had spent about three hours a week together. Wood was summoned to the jail to see if he could identify Holt as Muenter. It had been nine years and Wood was unsure. "The resemblance would be almost conclusive except that Muenter spoke quickly and clearly . . . he may be purposely changing his way of talking to avoid identification as Muenter."[8]

Frank was steadfast in his denial. He was not Erich Muenter. The *Washington Times* headline would read, "Holt Laughs at Story That He Is Muenter."[9]

The theory that Holt was part of a larger conspiracy of pro-German operatives continued to gain traction. Tunney, by now, knew the finances just didn't add up, and the previously talkative Holt refused to discuss them. How could he possibly afford to purchase 120 pounds of dynamite sold at ten dollars a stick and two guns?

Holt was no ordinary defendant and he had three attorneys to prove it: Martin Littleton, an attorney who represented the putatively insane murderer Harry Thaw, was retained by Frank's father-in-law. Two other attorneys were on Frank's team, Thomas J. Reidy and Edward R. Koch, most likely retained by Cornell professors. The three conferred at the courthouse in Mineola.

Holt complained to the warden that the jailers were disrespectful to him by calling him by his first name, and he requested that they be told to address him as Mr. Holt. The newspaper accounts of the Morgan shooting met with Holt's approval and were "very satisfactory."[10] He found it necessary to clarify the source of the cartoon of the figure of Lady Columbia and Uncle Sam was *not* from the *Philadelphia Public Ledger* but the *Philadelphia Record.*

Frank felt he needed to send his wife a foreboding message.

> Glad you are well, but after what has happened I do not wish to live longer. I trust you will bring up our little ones to love and fear God.
> FRANK[11]

•

In Washington, DC, the detectives continued to investigate the bombing and scoured the streets for possible witnesses to the Capitol bombing. They traced the bomber's every movement, but he'd exhibited remarkable skill in covering his tracks.

On July 4, Prof. Charles E. Munroe had been summoned to the Capitol to conduct a forensic investigation into the source and type of explosive and the manner of detonation. Munroe had earned his reputation as the inventor of smokeless powder and creator of the "Munroe effect," a device shaped to create more powerful explosions in a concentrated environment. When Munroe entered the Senate Reception Room, it was filled with the smell of smoke and doused fire. Munroe filtered the debris through a sieve painstakingly for hours. He hunted through the tangled wood, wire, plaster, and glass, searching for any bit of metal associated with the explosive. After he inspected the smallest of particles, he ordered the police to load the piles of debris and cart them off to his laboratory. Early reports had concluded that it was not a natural gas explosion. There was no gas in that area of the Capitol.

After examining the explosives, Munroe concluded that this incendiary bomb employed a state-of-the-art technique made with "chloride-of-silver cell,"[12] an ideal blasting tool.

Dr. Munroe persisted in his laboratory analysis of the type of explosive used, how it was ignited, and the timer.

Professor Munroe concluded that a sophisticated timed device had detonated the bomb. Components of the bomb were still not found. At a Senate hearing, about a year later, Professor Munroe testified that "Mr. Holt used dynamite, and he used a peculiar bomb, the most remarkable bomb that has ever been devised; and to think of its being devised by a professor of languages."[13]

Holt's confession about exploding dynamite with match caps, he opined, was impossible. After Professor Munroe gained access to Holt's cabin in Central Park, he found copper capsule detonators, a vastly more sophisticated mechanism for detonating a bomb.

When newsmen asked the German Embassy in Washington to provide a statement about the German-born man who shot J. P. Morgan, Prince Von Hatzfeldt Trachtenberg, of the German Embassy, refused, official or otherwise, to comment about this crime, Morgan, or any possible German conspiracy.

•

Then more evidence appeared that supported Tunney's conspiracy theory. Sir Cecil and his wife left Matinicock. Walter Paddison, a Morgan chauffer, drove them to the home of Willard D. Straight, a partner at Morgan & Co. Straight, and his wife, the former Dorothy Payne Whitney. En route to the Straight home, about four miles south from the Morgan estate, a dark-colored touring car blocked Paddison's vehicle. Six men exited the touring car and stood across the road with arms outstretched, making a human chain. With daring aggression, Paddison accelerated and aimed directly at two of the men. The six fled.

Sir Cecil appeared unaffected and never said a word to Straight upon his arrival. When a reporter telephoned Straight about the incident, he was shocked. "The English are by nature self-controlled, but I should imagine Sir Cecil would have mentioned the affair at least had he known that he had just escaped a hold-up."[14] An investigation provided no conclusion as to who obstructed the car.

•

Tunney continued his focus on the Keystone Powder Company from the markings on the dynamite in Frank's pocket and found on the Morgan estate. He contacted the company, and their records indicated that two hundred sticks of dynamite were delivered to the Syosset stationhouse. Tunney was back on Long Island to interview George D. Carnes, the station agent. Carnes described a man named Henderson, who received the packages and trunks and told Carnes he needed the explosives to blow up some tree stumps. When the packages and trunks arrived, he signed as Frank Hendrix. Carnes had no further information as to the location of the trunks of explosives but provided Tunney with all the receipts. Tunney tracked the trunks from Central Park to their last shipping point on July 2—Pennsylvania Railroad Station. Tunney had his squad check for the dynamite at the Pennsylvania Station but learned the items were picked up and moved—location unknown. Now Tunney was combing Holt's whereabouts in Central Park to find out where those trunks of dynamite were stored and any information he could ascertain.

The locals were readily forthcoming about the shanty in the woods where Frank had been staying. Outside the door was a charred dynamite box and some waxed-paper wrappers from sticks of dynamite. There was evidence that something was burned but no dynamite. The possibility of an impending dynamite explosion weighed heavily on Tunney's mind.

Tunney drove Carnes back to Mineola to identify Frank Holt as Henderson/Hendrix. Tunney confronted the prisoner: "Look here, I have the number of the check. The dynamite is in the trunk. It's liable to go off any minute and kill a lot of people. I can trace that check, but it will take time, and you better tell me quick where you left the trunk."[15]

Frank's every action seemed to be calculated and premeditated and served his own cause. Tunney was closing in. Perhaps out of fear of a massive and indiscriminate explosion thoroughly discrediting either a message of peace or a clandestine program of sabotage of hidden targets, Frank said, "All right."[16] He described a storehouse somewhere near 40th Street and 7th Avenue.

Twenty-eight minutes later, Tunney and a lieutenant were on 40th Street. They located an empty storage office. This led them to a warehouse on 38th Street. An old watchman was visibly shaken by the news of the dynamite stored in a trunk in the warehouse. New York City Police commissioner got word about a possible location of a trunk full of explosives and called with the directive—get it and get it fast. Unfortunately, there were floors of trunks stacked six-feet high. They were searching for a needle in a haystack. It was an impossible task for one or two police officers, even those who were expert in explosives. Tunney ordered as many police as could be spared to help race against time.

•

The question of Holt's identity haunted many, including Erich Muenter's family in Chicago. The *Chicago Daily Tribune* front-page story reran two pictures, one of Frank Holt and the other of Erich Muenter, with the banner line, "Are These Pictures of the Same Man?"[17]

Muenter's sisters Bertha and Louise had a change of heart and told the press that the man in custody was their brother. Their sister Agnes disagreed. The siblings would keep the news from their mother. Bertha said, "I'm afraid it would kill her. She will never know of the Morgan shooting if I can prevent it."[18]

Tips pouring into the police and press about the dual identity were the usual mix of guesswork, wishful thinking, fantasy, and plausible fragments of information. A Baltimore physician told the *New York Times* that, in 1906, a man by the name of Frank Holt, who he believed was Erich Muenter, acted as his interpreter. Holt, he said, had interpreted for his Finnish patients. He told the physician that when he was a child, his family was driven to emigrate from Finland because of Russian persecutions. Holt also translated signs posted in the hospital into seven languages. The physician recalled that Holt had undergone surgeries in Baltimore for an affliction that left scars on his body.

•

In Cambridge, newsmen were pursuing the local angle on the national story, with the intent on proving that Holt was Muenter. One newspaper paid the travel expenses of Charles R. Apted, the assistant superintendent of buildings at Cambridge, to visit the jail in Mineola. Apted knew Muenter well and was convinced that he could identify him despite the passage of nine years.

When he arrived in Mineola, Frank's condition had deteriorated.

In response to Apted's question, the prisoner mumbled an indistinct answer and closed his eyes. Apted knew that questioning the man would be fruitless, and he left after only a few minutes, unable to make an identification.

•

The only issue for William J. Corcoran, district attorney of Middlesex County in Cambridge, Massachusetts, was a positive identification of Holt as Muenter that would be ironclad for a jury. He announced that Theodore W. Hiller, who resided in the same house as Muenter, would be a reliable and qualified person to determine if Holt was Muenter. A positive identification would permit the immediate start of extradition proceedings to remove the suspect to Massachusetts. State Det. Silas P. Smith would also travel to Mineola to identify the prisoner as Muenter.

The indictment against Muenter preceded his New York arrest, and the Massachusetts's charge was a capital offense punishable by death. Massachusetts had a good shot at winning the jurisdictional jockeying for position.

Nine years before District Attorney George A. Sanderson had been denied a finding of murder at the inquest conducted by Judge Almy. Sanderson did not stop there. Less than one month after the inquest, Sanderson convened a grand jury of twenty-three Cambridge citizens to listen to the details of the how Leone died nine days after childbirth. He subpoenaed the cast of witnesses who testified before Judge Almy. The doctors, medical examiner, and pathologist described with great detail the grave situation they witnessed. The grand jurors were not persuaded by Edith Chase's homage to a savvy, shrewd professor.

By the time the grand jury convened, there was circumstantial evidence that Erich purchased a deadly, white, odorless powder or crystal, corrosive sublimate at the local drugstore. He fed his wife beef tea laced with arsenic and possibly a tad of corrosive sublimate, which caused her to die a slow, agonizing, and painful death. The grand jury had little trouble seeing through the ruse that the victim's Christian Science beliefs denied her life-saving care.

Ultimately, the grand jury found probable cause to believe that the Harvard scholar committed the crime of murder. They returned an indictment.

District Attorney Sanderson did not disclose the sealed indictment to the press. The proceedings of a grand jury are secret and an indictment is usually not disclosed until the named defendant is apprehended. But a warrant was issued for the arrest of Erich Muenter. Sanderson would not have the opportunity to prosecute Erich Muenter because in 1907 he became a judge of the Massachusetts Superior Court.

Cambridge Chief Inspector Hurley stated that the signed original indictment had been missing since it was requested in August 1914, when the New York Life Insurance Company had made an inquiry. The insurer had received a claim for the $1,000 insurance money. The missing file should have contained the indictment signed by the foreman. "The 'filler' or descriptive part, was removed and the 'baker' or envelope returned to its place in the files. Its disappearance would not have been revealed by a cursory examination of the files."[19] A limited number of people had access to the file. District Attorney Corcoran admitted it was strange that the indictment was missing. He believed it had been stolen.

Fortunately for Corcoran, a second copy of the indictment was kept in the court records.

Now that Muenter was again front and center in the public eye, Corcoran claimed that his office had been pursuing Muenter nonstop over at least the past eight months, but that Muenter had eluded them. There had been a $1,000 reward for information leading to the arrest of Erich Muenter.

•

One would expect that the news of the dual identity of Frank Holt would have rocked the Sensabaugh family to its core. A family decision was made that because the identification was unconfirmed and a matter of speculation, it did not require comment. The family had a more immediate issue to address. Secret Service agents were sent to the Sensabaugh home to speak with Mrs. Holt. The bombing of the Capitol and Frank's possession of substantial amounts of dynamite had become a matter of national urgency.

Leona received another letter from Frank:

> My Dear Darling:
> You are the only one I can and must trust and entrust with this news. I know you are strong in your faith for God and love for your fello-men, and do therefore approve of my action. The fact that it should strike our family instead of John Smith's may seem hard, but can't be helped. One hundred times, I said, like Jonah, 'Lord, send somebody else,' but I got only one an-

> swer. Nobody else seems to be available. I have prayed and trembled and doubted and lain awake at night and thought and thought, but there is no way out of it. The slaughter in Europe must be stopped and America must stop sending ammunition. If it goes on, I cannot live, for I am responsible in so far that I do not stop it when I can. But I will try.[20]

•

When the Cornell faculty read the news that Frank Holt was most probably the Harvard professor who poisoned his wife, it seemed to unnerve those who knew his true identity. There was the possibility now that they would be found out. Cornell Prof. C. W. Bennett, whom Frank had approached about forming a chapter of the Acacia fraternity, now came forward to reveal that when Professor Gould of the University of Chicago visited Cornell, Gould told Bennett that Frank Holt was the murder suspect Erich Muenter. At the time of Gould's visit, Bennett pledged his silence to Gould for unknown reasons. The press was clamoring for information from Gould, but he was not forthcoming.

CHAPTER 26

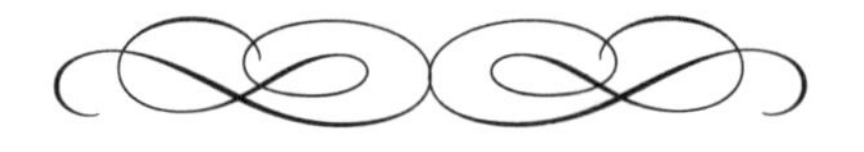

July 6

134 Sticks of 60 Percent Dynamite

In Mineola, evidence was mounting that the man who called himself Holt, when he wasn't claiming to be Totten, Hendrix, Henderson, Pearce, or Lester, was the missing fugitive, Muenter, from 1906.

At around this time, the prisoner received a telegram from his wife:

> Have best counsel here. Advised to rest and wait, and you must do the same. Send loving greetings hourly. Beautiful tribute to you in both evening papers here. I am tarrying for details of finances. I will come when you need me. Do not be afraid. Rest.
> Leona[1]

Leona, the twenty-eight-year-old wife, mother of two, and a devout person of faith, was resolute in her loyalty to her husband despite the news that he had bombed the Capitol and shot J. P. Morgan. But now there was the nearly confirmed report that her husband was Erich Muenter, a murderer, who had abandoned two small children. The messenger-of-peace narrative could not be stretched to shroud a horrifically painful murder with no apparent motive. If true, he had lied to her about every detail of his life prior to meeting her seven years ago.

Early in the day, the prisoner revealed to Tunney that he had lied about assembling the bomb in Washington. He now claimed he made the bomb in the Central Park bungalow. He admitted to receiving a shipment of 120 pounds of dynamite and continued to maintain that he would reveal all further details on Wednesday, July 7.

Constable Frank McCahill visited the cottage that the man named Totten had rented in Central Park. In the shambles was a pamphlet giving information about the New York Public Library and the offices of the *Staats-Zeitung* German newspaper. The newspaper promptly issued a statement that they had no communication with the man under either the name Holt or Muenter.

Alienists Dr. Carter MacDonald and Dr. Austin Flint were summoned to administer a complete mental examination of the prisoner to determine if he was competent to participate at the hearing the next day.

•

At his home in Chicago, Erich Muenter's longtime friend and former neighbor, Professor Crowe, came forward with crucial information that could end the debate over the prisoner's true identity. He said that Muenter had scars "left by repeated operations for a chronic malady, which would show on Holt if he is the same person."[2] Crowe then provided Erich Muenter's background. He was born and educated in Uelzen, Germany, a town known as the beet capital of the world. He has three sisters. In Germany, he attended the Gymnasium, a school with a special focus on foreign languages. In 1889, eighteen-year-old Erich arrived in the United States with his parents and three sisters and lived for a time in Fort Worth and other Texas towns. The family found their way to the German community in Chicago. In 1895 he entered the University of Chicago and received a bachelor of arts degree four years later. While studying at the university he taught French and German at Racine College and Kenwood Preparatory School in Chicago.

Recalling the time Crowe and his wife lived in the same building as Erich and Leone in Chicago, Crowe said, "He was brilliant and a tireless student. Stories that he attempted to asphyxiate his wife I do not believe."[3] The reporter pressed for more details. For the first time Crowe would disclose details about the gas incidents. He said there were three instances. His recollection was that he lived in a separate flat in the same building and Erich came charging into his flat.

> "Save her! he shouted to me: 'save her, she's dying. The wind blew out the gas.' . . . I put my hand to turn off the jet and found it already turned off. The window was open. The woman was almost unconscious on the bed. I calmed him and got him to call a doctor while I moved her arms up and down, and did other things to bring on artificial respiration. Muenter was not shamming grief and anxiety. His voice trembled when he got the doctor on the wire and his wife, opened her eyes and looked at him I could see that he was happy. I am sure the gas stories, therefore, are untrue."[4]

Crowe's version had the obvious contradiction of Leone's unconsciousness due to gas inhalation while the window was open.

Professor Gould of the University of Chicago would also now come forward and admit he had kept Muenter's identity secret. In 1906 he refused to accept evidence that Erich poisoned his wife. Erich could not possibly have been a murderer; his conversations about academic subjects were sophisticated, knowledgeable, and beyond reproach, at a level most academics or other professionals and certainly no common folk would be able to comprehend.

It had been less than a year, in November, since Gould met with Frank at Cornell.

Gould told the press for reasons of personal safety he would not expose the man. But fear was not his only motive; he was content knowing that Erich seemed to have prospered.

Gould said, "The newspapers of Chicago have begun hounding me and I think it better policy to say nothing further."[5]

•

Ottmar M. Krembs, Leone's older brother, would travel to Mineola to identify the prisoner as his sister's murderer. He would bring several photographs of Erich at a point in his life when he was not sporting his trademark beard. He believed the likeness between the pictures of the smooth-faced Muenter and those of Holt were strikingly similar.

Ottmar was convinced the prisoner was his missing brother-in-law and was confident justice would be served for the murderer of young Leone Krembs. "I am glad under the laws of Massachusetts he can be electrocuted for murder."[6] Leone's mother was distraught that her fugitive son-in-law had struck again after taking her daughter's life.

Leone and Erich's two little girls were thirteen and nine years old.

Prestigious institutions that had previously employed Frank felt an obligation to make a statement lest they be disparaged. It had been three years since Frank Holt taught at Emory and Henry College. Prof. A. G. Williams said of the man he knew as Holt, "He was scholarly, but eccentric, and very odd in his manner. He had an utter abhorrence of bloodshed, and his hallucination about stopping the war must have come from a supersensitiveness."[7]

•

Newsmen continued to monitor Jack Morgan's condition with the other stories surrounding Frank Holt. No further reports on the condition of J. P. Morgan had been issued since the day of the shooting. After conferring with his father's doctors, Junius Morgan issued an upbeat statement: "We can hardly keep him in bed. He slept eight hours last night and enjoys his cigars as much as he ever did."[8] Junius also said that his father's wishes were that the prisoner be committed to an insane asylum.

Jack called the firm and discussed business and was at his desk at home working most of the day. It was reported that he had a good appetite and no fever.

When the reporter told Junius of the findings of evidence of dynamite and target practice at Central Park, Junius didn't hesitate: "Go to it. You have my best wishes."[9]

•

At the Nassau County Jail, Dr. Cleghorn examined the prisoner for the surgical scars that Crowe had described. The physician confirmed that the scars on Frank Holt's lower back were identical to the scars on Erich Muenter.

The headline in the *Dallas Daily Times Herald* said it all: "Scars on Holt's Body Said to Correspond to Muenter's Description."[10]

In an audacious attempt to spin the bad news, Reverend Sensabaugh told the reporters, "If Holt really was a man who had dropped to life's bottom—and I can't believe it—I take my hat off to him for the way he came back."[11] The reverend, a forgiving man, may have been alone in wanting to tip his hat to a murderer who inflicted gruesome pain on his victim, with the first name strangely similar to his own daughter's.

The reverend reported that his daughter was in a "serious condition."[12] She was confined to her room, and anyone who spoke with Leona was prohibited from providing news of her husband's other identity, but she, of course, had already learned of the news.

Judge Cockrell provided the press with a part of a letter written by Frank to Leona. It was postmarked July 3. Frank detailed a version of how the Capitol bomb was made and his plan to take the Morgan family as hostages. Judge Cockrell spun the facts as best he could.

•

In Washington, DC, Prof. Charles Munroe, the expert on explosives, held a press conference and demonstrated both trick matches and regular matches soaked in sulfuric acid. As described by the prisoner, the upside-down bottle held sulfuric acid with a cork for two days. The acid never ate through the cork, nor did the matches ignite the acid. Based on the masses of debris Munroe found at the scene, he concluded that the blast had been caused by dynamite or an explosive charge and not gunpowder, as the prisoner described. There were no burn marks left where the explosion occurred. He pieced together the puzzle and hypothesized the sophisticated yet inchoate theory that the bomber "squeezed the fulminate composition out from the detonators, and then he had inserted that composition in the cavity he made in the stick of dynamite."[13]

Based on the extensive damage to the room and the building, Munroe decided that high explosives were used. Munroe believed the damage would have been worse but for an opened window and the arch leading to the Senate hallway, which released some of the force from the explosion. This was not the work of a lone novice; a sophisticated craftsman was behind the bomb—and one who was intent on destruction.

•

On the afternoon of July 6, a letter from Frank reached Leona in Dallas, providing details of the next planned disaster.

> My Dear Darling:
> You are the only one I can and must trust and entrust with this news.
>
> The steamer leaving New York for Liverpool on July 8 should sink, God willing, on the 7th; I think it is the Philadelphia or Saxonia, but am not quite sure, as according to schedule, these two left the 3rd.

[On the margin of the letter Frank wrote: "Tear this off until after it happens."]

Your affectionate FRANK[14]

Leona's initial reaction was to honor her husband's confidence in her. She was inclined to stand by her husband, but there would be serious consequences to her and her children by keeping a looming catastrophe a secret. The SS *Philadelphia* accommodated 1,700 passengers and 300 crew. The RMS *Saxonia* of the Cunard line had rooms for 1,900 passengers. Both ships left the New York harbor on Saturday, July 3. Why was Frank willing to share with her news of a planned bombing of ships?

For the first time, Leona broke with her husband and revealed to her father only the part of the letter describing the expected sinking of a ship. Reverend Sensabaugh, who had been a staunch supporter of his son-in-law, could not remain silent. He had both a moral and legal responsibility to protect innocent victims from death. He contacted a family friend, a former Texas governor, who without a second of delay, transmitted the information to the US Department of the Navy.

•

At the Mineola jail Frank's condition continued to deteriorate. Jeremiah Ryan was ordered by the warden to guard Frank Holt during the evening hours. He was posted outside the cell. The cell door was unlocked for easy access in case of another suicide attempt. Ryan's recounting of the facts would be challenged and questioned. He believed the prisoner was asleep when he heard a loud noise at the far end of the prison. He left his post to investigate the noise. The prisoner crept out of his cell to the end of the corridor, climbed up the crossbars about twenty feet, and jumped headfirst onto the cement floor. When Ryan returned, he found Frank's body lying in a pool of blood. Ryan immediately alerted the jail physician and District Attorney Smith. Early news reports claimed Frank had been shot by a German operative. Others, like Tunney, would speculate that Ryan never left his post but possibly had too many spirits with his dinner and fell asleep.

Coroner Walter R. Jones issued the following statement: "Undoubtedly a suicide and undoubtedly the man jumped. I cannot give an official version until an autopsy is performed by the jail physician, Doctor Cleghorn."[15]

The body was taken to the morgue.

•

The search of the Manhattan warehouse continued feverishly into the night. Police and Bomb Squad members spent hours opening trunks, boxes, and crates, knowing that their own lives could be ended with a sudden dynamite explosion. According to Tunney's calculation, there would be enough dynamite to blow up an entire New York City square block and reduce it to a pile of ash. Each floor of the warehouse had little or no light to aid the officers' search.

After hours of searching, on the top floor of a five-story warehouse, buried among hundreds of trunks, they found "the biggest seizure of explosives intended for illegal purposes."[16] The trunk contained 134 sticks of 60 percent dynamite, a box of blasting caps and powder, sulfuric acid, and matches. Along with the dynamite were packed nails, hammer, bolts, and other tools. According to Tunney, the trunk with explosives needed to be "hauled out, snake[d] across other piles, and carried down four flights of steep stairs in the dark to the office."[17]

Tunney was fastidious in accounting for all of the late prisoner's dynamite. Fifty sticks were still missing, an equivalent of thirty pounds of dynamite. Tunney called the commissioner.

CHAPTER 27

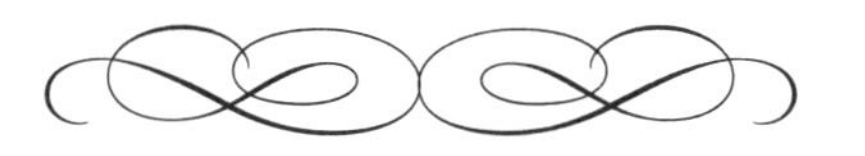

July 7

SS Minnehaha

In the medical examiner's office, Dr. Cleghorn conducted an autopsy and once again confirmed that Frank Holt was Erich Muenter. This did not stop Leona from contacting Cleghorn and directing him to send Frank's body to Ithaca, New York, where he would be buried.

For the first time since her husband's notoriety surfaced, Leona left her room. She was composed and calm and met with reporters from the *Times Herald* and *Associated Press.* She was accompanied by her two-year-old son, Oscar. Judge Cockrell and her father were by her side. According to the *Times Herald,* she was without a tear or sob. She thanked the *Times Herald* for the favorable editorial of her husband printed on July 5. Apparently, her desire for favorable press treatment of Frank had not diminished. She acknowledged the seriousness of the letter she received concerning bombs planted aboard ships and assured all of her own innocence. "The proper authorities were notified immediately."[1]

The national news reported in the past several weeks that bombs had been detonated aboard nine ships in the New York harbor. All the ships were loaded at the Fabre Piers, Brooklyn, adjoining the piers used by the German Hamburg-American lines.

Leona ignored the revelation of her husband's dual identity. Reverend Sensabaugh preempted the press by answering the question on everyone's mind. "My daughter also refuses to believe Holt and Muenter are the same man."[2] Leona would never admit Holt's other identity.

•

After completing, the autopsy, Dr. Cleghorn described the brain as unusually large and heavy. It would be removed for study by alienists. The body was stored at the morgue in Hempstead. The cause of death was listed as "Fracture of the skull."[3] Capt. Silas P. Smith of the Cambridge state detective office examined the body, along with Theodore W. Hiller, and newsman A. T. Brown. They were armed with handwriting samples of Erich from his application to the University of Kansas, his dental records of bridgework and fillings, and his Bertillon measurements, a system of measurements of certain bony portions of the body. And there were the previously described scars. Nassau County District Attorney Lewis J. Smith announced that the decedent, identified as Frank Holt, was without any doubt Erich Muenter. The Nassau County Medical Examiner's office gave an official statement that Frank Holt and Erich Muenter were the same person.

After learning of the statement, Ottmar Krembs, Leone's brother, inexplicably told the press, "We did not bear any ill will to Muenter."[4] The Krembs family were at a loss to comment on Erich's new family in Dallas, Texas.

Bertha Muenter, Erich's sister, who probably knew much more than she let on, wanted to end the speculation and questioning. She again said, "That is my brother Erich. There is no doubt of it."[5]

•

More confirmations of Holt's true identity came from around the county. In Cambridge, Harvard Prof. Hugo Münsterberg made a surprising revelation to the press. He told reporters, "I knew that Frank Holt and Erich Muenter were the same man as soon as I saw the pictures in the newspapers."[6] During Erich's time at Harvard, he was a frequent visitor to Münsterberg's classroom and borrowed many books on insanity.

The reporter asked, "Do you think overstudy on this morbid subject weakened his mind?"[7]

His response was, "No, I think he was a pathological study before he came to this country. The man was always interested in mysticism and metaphysics."[8]

It was the headline in a Dallas newspaper that reigned terror in the public. "Two Ships and Thousand People Menaced by Holt."[9] The US

Navy had utilized a combination of wireless communication and speedboats to alert ships believed to be carrying the explosive device referred to in Holt's letter. Frank Holt may have struck again either single-handedly, or as Tunney predicted at the direction of a German spy commander. The US Navy labeled the information high priority.

•

On Wednesday, July 7, The SS *Minnehaha* had been sailing for three days from New York on its way to Liverpool. Suddenly, at 3 P.M., the no. 3 hold carrying 15,000 tons of ammunitions and cargo exploded. Flames engulfed the hold. Two sailors were hurled into the air. The ship's alarm was activated and the crew were ordered to begin emergency procedures to douse the flames, save the ship from sinking, and prevent the fire from traveling to the ammunitions on board.

The captain sent a message at 5 P.M. via wireless that the ship's location was 570 miles southeast of Halifax, Nova Scotia. The ship had a crew of about one hundred and no passengers. The captain notified its owners, International Mercantile Marine (IMM), owned by Morgan interests.

The ship's status was tenuous. The crew struggled for two days, day and night. The harbor master of the landing pier at Halifax ordered the SS *Minnehaha* not to proceed to the pier due to the danger the vessel posed to other ships.

The captain was determined to steer the distressed ship with the contained fire through the mist and rain to Halifax.

Elaborate measures had been taken before the *Minnehaha* set sail from New York to guard against saboteurs, but obviously some person or persons planted the explosives on board.

Frank prophesied in his letter to Leona about the sinking of the ships *Philadelphia* or *Saxonia*. Was this a calculated ruse to divert attention away from ships carrying munitions? Was he a German saboteur who had pledged to die by suicide after carrying out heinous crimes?

Authorities investigated whether this was the handiwork of the now-deceased prisoner, but no hard proof linked him to the bombing. Holt promised all would be made clear on July 7. What the explosion on the *Minnehaha* made clear was that Holt's capture and death would not be the end of German sabotage.

Detectives were now taking seriously any messages regarding explosives or murder attempts. Police were scouring New Orleans to find the author Pearce, who had sent a new letter to the local newspaper. He wrote, "Holt (Muenter) was my partner. We worked together ever since this cursed war began. Holt is gone but I am still here, and I am going to carry on the work the two of us began. I am going to carry on the work with redoubled fury."[10]

CHAPTER 28

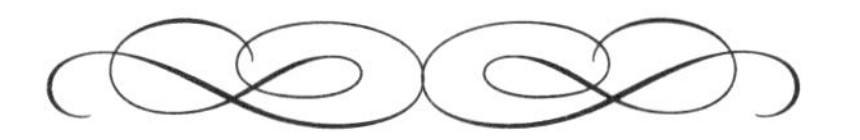

Frank Holt

Leona had a change of heart and decided she wanted her husband to be buried in Dallas. She believed it would be undignified and indecent for her husband to be buried in obscurity. Leona continued to avoid addressing her husband's growing litany of crimes. Her husband, the father of her children, and the kind, decent man and first-class scholar should not be treated as a common criminal. She sent a telegram to Dr. Cleghorn to prepare the body for its journey to Texas. All expenses would be defrayed by her family. She provided Dr. Cleghorn with the following information for the death certificate: Name: Frank Holt, native of Wisconsin, born near Milwaukee on March 25, 1875. Cleghorn, who had confirmed the identity of Frank Holt as Erich Muenter, prepared a death certificate with the fictitious name and information provided by Leona.

Undertaker George Brewer and the Sensabaugh family would receive the remains. The public's curiosity over the case would end in Dallas. No information regarding funeral plans was disclosed. Eventually, information leaked that the body would arrive on the four o'clock train in the afternoon, over the Frisco railroad. The interment would be at Grove Hill Cemetery.

Cleghorn's responsibilities in this case would not end with the shipping of the decedent to Dallas. An inquest was scheduled at the courthouse into the death of Frank Holt, aka Erich Muenter, and Cleghorn was called to testify.

Conspiracy theories quickly gathered even though there was a growing suspicion that the suicide occurred because of Jeremiah Ryan's laxity.

Ryan testified that Warden William Hult told him, "Don't leave him a moment, Jerry, watch him carefully. I said 'I will Bill, I will watch him as close as I can.'"[1] He admitted that he disobeyed those orders when he left his post to investigate a noise in another part of the jail. The details about the noise were never questioned. Some speculated Frank pretended he was asleep and set up a decoy to get Ryan away from his post. Ryan testified that when he returned to his post, he almost stumbled on Holt's body. Assistant District Attorney Weekes asked Ryan, who was sixty-four years old, if at any time he fell asleep. Ryan emphatically denied the insinuation. Ryan admitted that he had one glass of beer with his dinner before going on duty. He also told reporters that he believed he was "framed."

Clarence Cornell, the undertaker, stated that there was no gunshot wound in the skull, and that there had been so much blood on the floor that it was necessary to put down planks to walk on. Death was caused by a cerebral hemorrhage and a fracture of the base and vault of the skull.

Cleghorn testified he was satisfied that Holt had jumped to his death. There were competing requests from Boston and New York City to hold the brain for a postmortem study, but after minimal examination, it had been sent with the prisoner's body to Dallas.

The Sensabaugh family procession was guarded by a cordon of "plain clothes men"[2] at the cemetery, where Frank was laid to rest at 5 P.M., a time purposely chosen to keep gawkers out of the cemetery. Photographers were threatened with arrest.

Newspaper accounts of the funeral held at Brewer's Chapel describe many Methodist and civic dignitaries attended the six o'clock in the evening interment at Grove Hill Cemetery. W. D. Bradfield, editor of the *Advocate,* conducted the service. J. P. Musset of Fort Worth delivered the eulogy. How does one eulogize such a man? Musset did so by extolling the Sensabaugh family for the courage with which they endured the tragedy.

The pallbearers at Frank Holt's funeral constituted an interesting group of Sensabaugh friends, including R. H. Shuttles (wholesale jeweler), S. J. Hay (former mayor of Dallas and one of the founders of Trinity Methodist Episcopal Church South, where he sometimes preached), and B. M. Burgher (postmaster and layman in Oaklawn Methodist).

Three clergymen from the Methodist Episcopal Church read prayers during the brief service. The only hymn was "Lead Kindly Light." Leona stood between her father and stepmother and showed no emotion. Two-year-old Oscar was held by his grandfather. After the funeral party dispersed, there was a continuous parade of curious onlookers who wished to see the resting place of the man who had put the nation's nerves on edge.

The headstone that remains in place to this day at Grove Hill Memorial Park reads "Doctor Frank Holt 1875–1915."

EPILOGUE

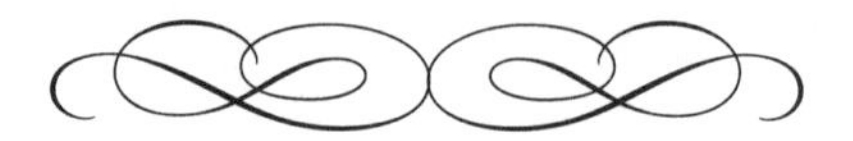

J. P. MORGAN

On August 16, 1915, forty-four days after he was shot, Jack returned to his desk at the Corner in New York's financial district. At 4:30 in the afternoon he walked out the door to thunderous applause from a waiting crowd. As he had done so many times before, he brushed off the press.

Jack was determined to keep the Morgan name out of the public eye after his father's death, but world events intervened following the attempted assassination. Gone were the days when Jack dismissed threats as "poppycock."[1] Fearing he was still a target, he hired former Marines as bodyguards for himself and his family and became more reclusive. Matinicock became an armed island with an entry guard on the bridge and guards along the shoreline of the Long Island Sound.

After the start of World War I, Jack fired all German and Austrian employees at Camp Uncas, a 4,000-square-foot log "cabin" on Lake Mohegan in the Adirondacks. Jack's sentiment was "licking Germany and the German people till they won't try it again."[2] Jack's son Junius served as a senior officer in the Great War.

Jack had hardened with time, and as he grew older, he held prejudices toward many. These prejudices were not well hidden. "Most of the Jews in the country are thoroughly pro-German, and a very large number of them are anti-J. P. Morgan & Co."[3] Jack objected to the appointment of Jews and Catholics to the governing board of Harvard University "The Jew is always a Jew first and an American second, and the Roman Catholic, I fear, too often a Papist first and an American second."[4] There was evidence of some softening of his prejudices in later years. He indirectly financed Jewish medical students at Harvard Medical School with small loans and gifts.

With the entry of the United States into the war on April 6, 1917, there was no longer a need for Morgan & Co. "credits." The United States granted the Allies $1 billion in credit. Two years and seven months later, the war ended. Jack sent a congratulatory note to King George V with the closing "God Save the King!"[5]

Years later, Jack said, "The fact that the Allies found us useful and valued our assistance in their task is the fact that I am most proud of in all my business life."[6] But there was more than sentimentality at play. Morgan & Co.'s credits to the Allies were a high risk but lucrative endeavor for Morgan & Co. and other bankers, who were to be repaid in gold-backed currency.

Germany's postwar reparations amounted to approximately $31.5 billion (today's value). Germany defaulted, and some reparations were deferred until the country's economy improved. Morgan's firm floated a loan for Germany.

Domestic threats and bombing continued even after the war. In May 1919, letter bombs addressed to Jack and twenty other Americans were intercepted by the Post Office. Jack's daughter, Jane, was extorted by a Michigan janitor, who claimed he poisoned her with slow-acting microbes and would provide the antidote for $22,000.

At the intersection of Wall and Broad Streets, the location of Morgan & Co., bankers, brokers, clerks, and back-office staff of brokerage houses and the stock exchange jammed the streets each day on their lunch break. On September 16, 1920, the Corner was the scene of a deadly attack. Unnoticed was an unmanned cart, drawn by a horse, in the street. Minutes later, an explosion caused hot iron shrapnel to rain on the pedestrians, killing more than thirty-eight and injuring three hundred. The new offices of Morgan & Co. were badly damaged. One Morgan employee died instantly in the bombing, another died a day later, and dozens were seriously injured. Junius, Jack's son, a Morgan partner, had lacerations from glass. Jack was in Scotland at the time. The bombers were never identified. Some speculated a small group of Italian anarchists was responsible. To this day, damage to the façade remains visible and unrepaired.[7] For eighty-one years the attack was unsurpassed in infamy until the Twin Towers fell on September 11, 2001.

•

Jack's paranoia reached a new height in 1920, when he hired a private detective to investigate a possible plot to destroy Morgan & Co. by members of the American Jewish community. But Jack, ever his father's son, never let down his guard in public. Jack followed his father's practices of hiring partners who were white, Protestant males. It wasn't until after World War II that Morgan & Co. hired its first Jewish employee.

In 1919, while vacationing in Rome, Jack provided a brief glimpse of self-reflection. "My special job is the most interesting I know of anywhere. More fun than being King, Pope, or Prime Minister anywhere—for no one can turn me out of it and I don't have to make any compromises with principles."[8]

Jessie, Jack's beloved wife and partner, died at age fifty-six in August 1925 after a short illness. The *New York Times* reporter quoted a neighbor as saying, "Mrs. Morgan was a great woman of dignity and charm. She was humane and friendly. She cared nothing for Long Island Society and her whole devotion was centered upon her family and eleven grandchildren."[9]

Jack never remarried. A few years later he bought another large waterfront property in Glen Cove and dedicated it to Jessie, calling it Morgan Memorial Park. He refused to accept any glory associated with his magnificent public gift. "I didn't want any dedication. Just open the gates of the park and let the people come in."[10] For over sixty-five years, locals have enjoyed its beach and summer-evening concerts.

Jack's mother died the year after Jessie.

•

In 1929 Jack Morgan and Owen Young, chairman of General Electric, were chosen as American delegates to a Paris conference to devise a solution to the German reparations issue. Jack cabled New York: "From what I see of the Germans they are 2nd-rate people and I would rather have their business done for them by someone else."[11]

David Sarnoff, who was born to a Jewish family in Belarus and later became president of RCA, brokered the deal reducing the schedule of reparation payments.

The perception of Jack as a positive force in global affairs was widely accepted. Princeton University bestowed an honorary doctor of laws degree upon Jack, stating that "He has helped in stabilizing the troubled affairs of the whole civilized world."[12]

Jack added four thousand books to his father's library. He continued to buy medieval, illuminated texts, utilizing the considerable expertise of Belle da Costa Greene. "My librarian told me she wouldn't dare spend so much of my money. But just the same, I wouldn't dare face her if I went home without the manuscripts."[13] Pierpont and then Jack relied on Belle's expertise in purchasing prized incunabula for his library. She continued as the director of the Morgan Library until her retirement in 1948, five years after Jack's death. In 1924 Morgan Library opened for limited public access.

•

In 1933 Jack must have felt life repeat itself. He was called to testify before the US Senate Committee on Banking and Currency, which was investigating "practices with respect to the buying and selling and the borrowing and lending" of stocks and securities.[14] Instead of Samuel Untermyer, it was Ferdinand Pecora, an aggressive, cigar-smoking former assistant district attorney from New York of Sicilian decent, whom Jack would call "a dirty little wop."[15] Jack referred to the House of Morgan as a private bank, the gentleman's bank with a heightened sense of ethics that surpassed any written code.

> The private banker is a member of a profession which has been practiced since the Middle Ages. In the process of time there has grown up a code of professional ethics and customs, on the observance of which depend his reputation, his fortune, and his usefulness to the community in which he works. Some private bankers, as indeed is the case in some of the other professions, are not as observant of this code as they should be; but if, in the exercise of his profession, the private banker disregards this code, which could never be expressed in legislation, but has a force far greater than any law, he will sacrifice his credit. This credit is his most valuable! possession; it is the result of years of fair and honorable dealing and, while it may be quickly lost, once lost cannot be restored for a long time, if ever.[16]

The hearings uncovered that neither Jack nor any other Morgan partner paid federal income tax for 1930, 1931, or 1932. The reason was sizable write-offs from stock losses, a concept that some in the hungry press called "tax evasion."[17]

Jack summed up the experience, saying, "The experience was extraordinarily trying and fatiguing. To have to stand before a crowd of people and attempt, by straight answers to crooked questions, to convince the world that one is honest, is a form of insult that I do not think would be possible in any civilized country. . . . I feel very deeply the injustice caused by the misuse of the Senatorial power of investigation, in that they only want to investigate for the purpose of satisfying public curiosity, and perhaps to get some more votes for their next election."[18]

But perhaps the lasting indignation that exists from the hearings is the photograph of a twenty-year-old Little Person, who was placed on his lap. Jack, assuming she was a child, is seen smiling at the Little Person. The press had a field day with references to the circus-like atmosphere.

In partial response to the Pecora hearings, Congress enacted the Glass-Steagall Act into law. Banks could not serve as both a commercial bank and underwriters of public securities. The bank giants had been slashed. Jack and his partners made the decision that Morgan & Co. would remain on the banking side and exit the underwriting business.

This led to the creation of the independent entity, Morgan Stanley, a firm founded by, among others, Henry Sturgis Morgan, Jack's son. Morgan Stanley prospered in the underwriting field.

And then in 1936, Jack would testify at the Nye hearings, the Senate Munitions Committee, which tried to uncover whether Americans who financially benefited from the Great War, had undue influence on the decision to enter the war in 1917.

•

As he aged, Jack lived a solitary life and never completely escaped the "blues" and loneliness. He did not change a thing after his wife died, including taking care of her garden. In later years he derived great pleasure from his grandchildren. "It makes a great difference to me in my life, which is necessarily very lonely."[19]

When he was at Matinicock, his family came for a formal dinner each Sunday. Jack's statement of ethical principles never changed. "Do your work; be honest; keep your word; help when you can; be fair."[20] His love for reading continued throughout his lifetime, changing from the classics to detective stories such as *The Adventures of Jimmy Dale* and *The Wire Devils.*

In June 1936, Jack suffered his first heart attack and developed severe neuritis, which made it difficult for him to walk. In a conversation later recalled by his friend Owen Young, Jack was despondent, lonely, and angry. He ranted to Owen how he didn't care what happened to him, anyone, or the country—only the business. He blustered that he wanted to take his business out of the country. Owen would temper his friend, noting that tears filled Jack's eyes as he expressed gratitude to Owen for his friendship.

•

Jack would live to see the Allies again at war with Germany. Jack had been infuriated with the peace-at-any price mentality of some Americans and British. When the United States entered World War II, both of Jack's sons became naval officers. On June 21, 1940, a year and a half before American entry in the war, Jack signed over the *Corsair IV* to the British Navy. He opened his home to three English children, refugees evacuated from British bombardment. German atrocities once again did not escape his condemnation. He wrote a friend, "I . . . regret to see your anti-Semitic feeling coming so strongly to the surface."[21] "As you know I am not very enthusiastic about Jews, but I must say that my heart is full of sympathy with those unfortunate people in Austria who suddenly find themselves outcasts after being respected and useful citizens, and outcasts deprived of all their property. It is more wicked than I thought anybody could be."[22]

In February 1940, Jack sold the New York Stock Exchange seat bought by his father forty-five years before. That same year, J. P. Morgan & Co. became a corporation. Jack explained in a press conference at Elphinstone: It was necessary because "so much of the capital is in a few hands, and those few hands are elderly. . . . the new laws render it impossible to make any money to replace the lost money quickly. . . . the stock will, I suppose, gradually get into the hands of the public. I only hope they will like it when they get it!"[23]

On February 3, 1942, J. P. Morgan & Co. went public. Smith, Barney & Co. bought 16,500 shares at $206 a share.

At the age of seventy-five, Jack suffered a heart attack en route to Florida. Two weeks later, on March 13, 1943, he died at the same age as his father, who had died thirty years earlier.

Papers were filled with commentary that was mostly flattering. Just like his father, he was described as the "financial titan."[24] The world knew him only as a somewhat "mysterious colossus of finance."[25]

According to Jack's grandson, Bob Pennoyer, he left an estate of less than $25 million. Pierpont's estate had been $78 million in 1913.

Matinicock on Morgan's Island was rented to the Soviet UN delegation in 1949. It was sold to an order of Catholic nuns and became a convent, which was later sold it to a developer. The Matinicock mansion was torn down and one hundred-forty homes were built on the island.

In 1949 the United Lutheran Church bought Jack's forty-five-room Madison Avenue townhouse for $245,000, then later sold it back to the Pierpont Library for $15 million.

Wall Hall became windowless as a result of the London Blitz. It was sold to the County Council and is now luxury apartments. The Morgan, Grenfell offices in London were also bombed. In the 1930s, the House of Morgan relinquished most of its control over the London office.

After Pierpont's death and Jack's ascendance to senior partner, one Morgan partner privately wrote about his skepticism, saying that he "had given no evidence of any such colossal personal force as his father had radiated."[26] Years later, a partner who had previously doubted Jack's abilities would say, "he was a great gentleman, a cultured gentleman. He was a simple and just as sweet a man as you ever saw never given credit, because he was shy. He wasn't a buccaneer like his father, but he was a hell of a guy."[27]

Today the name Morgan is just as recognizable in the world of banking and finance as it was more than one hundred years ago.

KREMBS FAMILY

The Krembs family has not forgotten the tragedy that befell one of their own many years ago. Steve Treanor is the Krembs family historian. While family members have lots of memories and memorabilia, none, of course, knew Leone, who died in 1906. So who was Leone Krembs? What did she think of Erich? So many questions about her life were unanswered until 2019, when Bill MacDonald, a Krembs relative, shared the diary and letters of Leone and the diary of her father, Moritz.

Here was Leone: her thoughts, dreams, and worries. Moritz's own diary revealed a father's pain upon learning of his daughter's death. But the most profound shock was the entry Moritz wrote about finding arsenic poisoning in Leone's newborn baby. This information was *never* revealed to the newspapers, police blotter, or court—Erich had directly, or through his wife, poisoned his wife and his newborn.

Bill MacDonald and his daughter had met baby Leone, named in honor of her mother, as an older woman, and he described her as a person of few words and limited abilities. Perhaps arsenic poisoning had taken a permanent toll on her health.

•

Helen was only three years old at the time of her mother's death and father's disappearance. She and her infant sister were initially adopted by their grandparents. They called their grandmother, Johanna Krembs, "Mother." Both Helen and baby Leone's surnames were changed from Muenter to Krembs.

In February 1907 Moritz's produce factory in Racine burned to the ground. It was a total loss. Three months later, and less than a year after Leone's death, Moritz died.

The family fell on hard, sad times. Helen was sent to live in Fond du lac, Wisconsin, with her grandmother's family. Because baby Leone needed more care, Louise, Leone's widowed sister, "adopted" baby Leone. Louise had a five-year-old daughter, Alma, who watched out for Leone and would do so for the rest of her life. Eighty-nine years after her mother's death, in 1996, baby Leone was buried at the same cemetery as her mother.

When asked about Helen, Steve Treanor wrote: "My soon to be 100-year-old mom never knew her despite her time in Chicago. She did know Louise, Alma, and Leone. Her comment about Louise was that she maintained an immaculate home and was always cleaning. Her comment about Leone was she was dependent on others and a bit odd."

Helen graduated with a bachelor of science degree from the University of Wisconsin and married Frederick K. Foster, an attorney. They adopted a son, Frederick. Helen and Fred seemed to be living separate lives at the time of her death. She was the head of an art department for a women's school in Vicksburg, Mississippi, when she died.

Steve Treanor wrote: "My assumption has always been that her career was very important to her and early childhood trauma likely instilled a certain independence in her. I have always thought it odd that she was buried in Mississippi rather than the family plot in Chicago and assume it was just part of her independent nature."

SENSABAUGH FAMILY

How Erich managed to meet and marry two women with almost the exact same first name is one of the many mysteries of his life.

As noted, Erich Muenter was buried in Grove Hill Cemetery, Dallas, under the fictitious name Frank Holt and an incorrect date of birth. Cornell never revoked his degree despite Muenter obtaining it under a false identity.

Leona and her two children, Oscar and Daisy, continued to live in her father's home and use the surname Holt. One month after the death of her husband, Leona enrolled in Southern Methodist University for the fall semester and received a master of arts degree. She moved to Greenville, Texas, and taught at Wesley College, then Alexander Collegiate Institute in Kilgore (later Lon Morris College) in Jacksonville, Texas.

In the spring of 1919, Leona was living with Oscar and Daisy in one of the college buildings. While Leona was on campus and her children in the dormitory building, six-year-old Oscar and five-year-old Daisy were using "canned heat," perhaps something akin to Sterno, to make candy. The liquid spilled on the front of Daisy's dress and she was consumed in fire. She died shortly after.[28]

Reverend Sensabaugh's memoir wrote only one sentence in tribute to his deceased granddaughter. He never mentions her older brother, his namesake, Oscar. Did the family blame the six-year-old for his sister's death?

Leona never acknowledged her husband's false identity, his prior marriage, his poisoning of his prior wife, his shooting of J. P. Morgan, the bombing of the US Capitol, or his potential role in the explosion on the *Minnehaha.*

Leona returned to SMU as a language instructor and then became acting dean of women. She never remarried and died on June 22, 1941, at the age of fifty-four and was buried in the same cemetery as her husband. Flags on the SMU campus flew at half-mast to honor her.

Her father, Rev. Oscar Fitzgerald Sensabaugh, died in Dallas on March 19, 1956.

Leona's son Oscar Holt became an aircraft engineer. He lived most of his life away from Dallas in Ohio.

The Krembs girls never met their half brother, Oscar.

NOTES

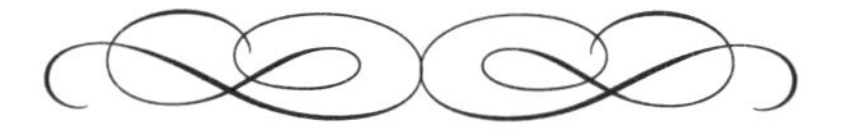

1. IT'S ALL OVER

1. "Last Days of Mrs. Muenter," *Boston Daily Globe,* Apr. 29, 1906, 1
2. "Last Days of Mrs. Muenter."
3. "Majestic Cathedral of Christian Science in Boston," *Boston Daily Globe,* Apr. 1, 1906, SM11.

2. GASTRO-DUODENITIS

1. Returns of a Death, Leone Krembs Muenter, Register No. 503, City of Cambridge, Commonwealth of Massachusetts, Apr. 15, 1906.

3. GOING HOME

1. Apr. 7, 1906, diary of Moritz Krembs, private papers of William MacDonald.
2. Undated letter, Lawrence, KS, Leone Muenter to Louise Krembs, private papers of William MacDonald.
3. "Muenter and Holt One, Says Writing Expert," *Washington Times,* July 7, 1915, 4.
4. Leone Muenter to Louise Krembs, July 5, 1905, private papers of William MacDonald.
5. Leone Muenter to Louise Krembs, July 5, 1905.

6. Leone Muenter to Louise Krembs, July 5, 1905.
7. Leone Muenter to Louise Krembs, July 5, 1905.
8. Letter of Louise Cramer, Dec. 12, 1905, private papers of William MacDonald.
9. "Murder Laid to Harvard Tutor," *Chicago Tribune,* Apr. 28, 1906, 1.
10. Orders, Rules and Regulations, The Commonwealth of Massachusetts, State Board of Registration in Embalming, Dec. 1917, 411–12, https://www.google.com/books/edition/Public_Documents_of_Massachusetts/71VBAQAAMAAJ?hl=en&gbpv=1&bsq=approved%20disinfectant.
11. Orders, Rules and Regulations.

4. LEONE'S SPIRIT

1. Leone Krembs, diary, 1893, private papers of William MacDonald.
2. "Father Says Tutor's Wife Was Murdered," *St. Louis Dispatch,* May 1, 1906, 2.

5. MONEY

1. *Chicago Tribune,* Apr. 19, 1906, 15.
2. "Krembs Bitter against Muenter," *Boston Daily Globe,* Apr. 29, 1906, 1.
3. Moritz Krembs, diary, Apr. 18, 1906, private papers of William MacDonald.
4. Leone Muenter to Louise Cramer, undated, private papers of William MacDonald.
5. Leone Muenter to Louise Cramer, undated.
6. Moritz Krembs, diary, Apr. 19, 1906, private papers of William MacDonald.
7. "Letter on Muenter Case," *North Adams (MA) Evening Transcript,* June 9, 1906, 3.

6. INHERITANCE POWDER

1. R. A. Witthaus and Tracy C. Becker, *Medical Jurisprudence, Forensic Medicine and Toxicology* (New York: W. Wood, 1896), 498.
2. Witthaus and Becker, *Medical Jurisprudence,* 498.
3. "Expressed Fear of Sudden Death," *Boston Daily Globe,* Dec. 30, 1905, 1.
4. "Mrs. Chase Died by Her Own Act," *Virginia Chronicle Evening Journal,* May 24, 1906, 8.
5. "Charge Murder," *Burlington (VT) Free Press and Times,* Apr. 28, 1906, 2.
6. "Murder Laid to Harvard Professor," *Chicago Daily Tribune,* Apr. 28, 1906, 1.
7. *Evening Herald* (Shenandoah, PA), Apr. 28, 1904, 4.
8. Moritz Krembs, diary, Apr. 26, 1906, private papers of William MacDonald.
9. Moritz Krembs, diary, Apr. 26, 1906.
10. "Scout Murder Charge," *Topeka Daily Capitol,* Apr. 28, 1906, 1.

11. "Muenter Accused of Murder of His Wife," *Boston Daily Globe,* Apr. 28, 1906, 1.
12. "Seek Harvard Teacher, Wife Murder Charge," *New York Times,* Apr. 28, 1906, 1.
13. "Muenter May Be in Monrovia," *Los Angeles Evening Express,* Apr. 30, 1906, 2.
14. "Muenter Accused of Murder," *Boston Daily Globe,* Apr. 28, 1906, 1.
15. "Murder Laid to Harvard Tutor," *Chicago Daily Tribune,* Apr. 28, 1906, 1.
16. "Muenter Accused of Murder of His Wife," *Boston Daily Globe,* Apr. 28, 1906, 1.
17. "Accuse an Old KU Tutor," *Kansas City Times,* Apr. 28, 1906, 1.
18. Erich Muenter, "Sensation! Scandal! Autopsy Cremation Assfixiation [*sic*]," Harvard College Library, June 6, 1906.
19. Muenter, "Sensation! Scandal! Autopsy Cremation Assfixiation [*sic*]."
20. Muenter, "Sensation! Scandal! Autopsy Cremation Assfixiation [*sic*]."

7. NEARED THE TRUTH

1. "Two More Women Say Holt Is Muenter," *San Francisco Examiner,* July 6, 1915, 2.
2. "Two More Women Say Holt Is Muenter."
3. "Urge Muenter to Return," *Chicago Daily Tribune,* May 1, 1906, 2.
4. "Muenter Accused of Murder of His Wife," *Boston Daily Globe,* Apr. 28, 1906, 1.
5. The Rosicrucian Cosmo-Conception, chapter 17, "The Method of Acquiring First-Hand Knowledge, The First Steps," https://www.rosicrucian.com/rcc/rcceng17.htm.
6. "Says Poison Is Mental," *Los Angeles Times,* May 7, 1907, 11.
7. "Mother Defends Her Son," *Los Angeles Evening Express,* May 1, 1906, 14.
8. "Says Poison Is Mental," 11.
9. Leone Muenter to Louise Cramer, undated, private papers of William MacDonald.
10. Mary Baker Eddy, *Science and Health, Key to the Scriptures,* chapter 10, https://www.christianscience.com/the-christian-science-pastor/science-and-health/key-to-the-scriptures.
11. Leone Muenter to Louise Cramer, July 1905, private papers of William MacDonald.

8. BERTHA

1. "Urge Muenter to Come Back at Once," *Boston Daily Globe,* May 1, 1906, 1.
2. "Urge Muenter to Come Back at Once."
3. "Refuses to See Police," *Boston Daily Globe,* Apr. 30, 1906, 1.
4. "Not Murder!," *Detroit Free Press,* May 3, 1906, 1.
5. *Detroit Free Press,* May 3, 1906, 2.
6. "Say Harvard Is Blocking Murder Probe," *St. Louis Post-Dispatch,* May 3, 1906, 11.

9. SHOCK AND SURPRISE

1. *Com. v. Mink,* 123 Mass. 422 (1877).

2. Returns of Medical Examiners, 1885–1960. Entry for Leone Krembs Muenter, v. 1906, pp. 658–59. SC1/series 166X. Massachusetts Archives. Boston, MA.

3. Return of a Death, Leone Krembs Muenter, Register No. 503, City of Cambridge, Commonwealth of Massachusetts, Apr. 15, 1906.

4. "Judge Refuses Warrant," *Baltimore Sun,* Apr. 29, 1906, 2.

5. Florence Nightengale, *Notes on Nursing* (London: Harrison, 1860), 102.

6. "Judge Refuses Warrant," 2.

7. "Think Muenter Is Second Johann Hoch," *Inter Ocean* (Chicago), Apr. 29, 1906, 5.

8. "Judge Refuses Warrant," 2.

9. "Last Days of Mrs. Muenter," *Boston Daily Globe,* Apr. 29, 1906, 1.

10. "Last Days of Mrs. Muenter."

11. "Last Days of Mrs. Muenter."

12. "Last Days of Mrs. Muenter."

13. Return of a Death, Leone Krembs Muenter, Register No. 503, City of Cambridge, Commonwealth of Massachusetts, Apr. 15, 1906.

14. Moritz Krembs, diary, May 11, 1906, private papers of William MacDonald.

15. Moritz Krembs, diary, May 12, 1906, private papers of William MacDonald.

10. POLYTECHNIC

1. Warren Schiff, "Germans in Mexican Trade and Industry During the Diaz Period," *The Americas* 23, no. 3 (1967): 293.

2. Classified ad 3, *New York Times,* Jan. 1, 1905, 20.

3. "San Benito, Texas," *Brownsville (TX) Daily Herald,* Oct. 25, 1909, 1.

4. "Polytechnic College," *Fort Worth Record,* Aug. 17, 1908, 5.

5. Risa Brown, *Polytechnic Days* (Birmingham, AL: Alliance Publishing, Feb. 26, 2020), 18.

6. *The Panther City Parrot Yearbook,* 1908, https://texashistory.unt.edu/ark:/67531/metapth627122/.

7. *Panther City Parrot Yearbook.*

11. MAY BE WOOED

1. "Poems Written by Frank Holt Showing His Morbid Tendency," *Ithaca Journal,* July 7, 1915, 1.

2. Rev. Oscar Sensabaugh, Memoir, Southern Methodist University Library Archives.

3. *The Panther City Parrot Yearbook,* 1909, https://texashistory.unt.edu/ark:/67531/metapth627122/.

4. *Panther City Parrot Yearbook.*

5. 1912–13 Emory & Henry catalog, Faculty and Instructors, Kelly Library, Emory & Henry College.

12. J. P. MORGAN

1. This book spells the name of J. P. Morgan's estate as *Matinicock* with two *i*'s, rather than the more common spelling with an *e* in place of the second *i.* If you travel to Long Island, you will see *Matinecock.* This work follows the spelling on the Morgan family embossed photo album located at the Morgan Library.

2. J. P. Morgan Jr. Papers, Box 233, Archives of the Pierpont Morgan Library, NY, Dec. 30, 1898, ARC 1216.

3. J. P. Morgan Jr. Papers, Box 233, Archives of the Pierpont Morgan Library, NY, Jan. 25, 1901, ARC 1216.

4. J. P. Morgan Jr. Papers, Box 233, Archives of the Pierpont Morgan Library, NY, ARC 1216 JPM to Mrs. JPM, Box 233, File 17.

5. Frances Morgan Pennoyer, interview by Robert M. Pennoyer, undated, private papers of Robert M. Pennoyer.

6. J. P. Morgan Jr. Papers, Box 233, Archives of the Pierpont Morgan Library, NY, Nov. 17, 25, 1898, ARC 1216.

7. Ron Chernow, *The House of Morgan* (New York: Grove Press, 2010), 112.

8. J. P. Morgan Jr. Papers, Box 233, Archives of the Pierpont Morgan Library, NY, June 18, 1901, ARC 1216.

9. J. P. Morgan Jr. Papers, Box 233, Archives of the Pierpont Morgan Library, NY, June 18, 1901, ARC 1216.

10. J. P. Morgan Jr. Papers, Box 4, Letterpress book 2, Archives of the Pierpont Morgan Library, NY, Dec. 19–23, 1907.

11. "Steel Terms Outline," *New York Tribune,* Mar. 3, 1901, 3.

13. YOUR LOVING SON, JACK

1. Jean Strouse, *Morgan: American Financier* (New York: Random House, 2012), 190.

2. John Douglas Forbes, *J. P. Morgan Jr. 1867–1943* (Charlottesville: Univ. Press of Virginia, 1981), 12.

3. Strouse, *Morgan,* 208.

4. J. P. Morgan Jr. Papers, Box 233, Archives of the Pierpont Morgan Library, NY, Oct. 29, Nov. 5 and 11, 1882, ARC 1216.

5. Chernow, *House of Morgan,* 263.

6. Strouse, *Morgan,* 209.

7. J. P. Morgan Jr. Papers, Box 233, Archives of the Pierpont Morgan Library, NY, June 4, 1884, ARC 1216.

8. J. P. Morgan Jr. Papers, Box 233, Archives of the Pierpont Morgan Library, NY, Apr. 4–15, May 6, Oct. 4, Nov. 15, 1883, ARC 1216.

9. J. P. Morgan Jr. Papers, Box 233, Archives of the Pierpont Morgan Library, NY, Jan. 18, 1889, ARC 1216.

10. William R. Huber, *George Westinghouse: Powering the World* (Jefferson, NC: McFarland & Company Inc., 2022), 115.

11. Frederick Lewis Allen, *The Great Pierpont Morgan* (New York: Dorset Press, 1989), 2.

12. Virginia Woolf, *Roger Fry* (New York: Harcourt, Brace and Company, 1940), 86.

14. HIS RETURN

1. Vincent P. Corosso, *The Morgans Private International Bankers 1854–1913* (Cambridge, MA: Harvard Univ. Press, 1987), 432.

2. J. P. Morgan Jr. Papers, Box 233, Archives of the Pierpont Morgan Library, NY, Jan. 3, 1905, ARC 1216.

3. *New York Times,* Nov. 10, 1907, SM9.

4. J. P. Morgan Jr. Papers, Box 233, Archives of the Pierpont Morgan Library, NY, Oct. 28, 1907, ARC 1216.

5. United States Senate Inquiry, Day 1, Testimony of Joseph Bruce Ismay, https://www.titanicinquiry.org/USInq/AmInq01Ismay01.php.

6. J. P. Morgan Jr. Papers, Box 8, Letterpress book 9, Archives of the Pierpont Morgan Library, NY, Apr. 26, 1912.

7. *Titanic* Inquiry Project, Report of the Committee on Commerce United States Senate, https://www.titanicinquiry.org/USInq/USReport/AmInqRep01.php.

15. AFTER MORGAN, WHO?

1. Louis D. Brandeis, *Other People's Money and How Bankers Use It* (New York: Frederick A. Stokes Company, 1913).

2. Brandeis, *Other People's Money,* 12.

3. Charles August Lindberg, *Banking and Currency and the Money Trust* (N.p.: C. A. Lindberg, 1913), 97, https://archive.org/details/pdfy-ly2qbyfaWtQyLoqw/mode/2up.

4. J. P. Morgan Jr. Papers, Box 8, Letterpress book 9:8, Archives of the Pierpont Morgan Library, NY, Apr. 25, 1912.

5. J. P. Morgan Jr. Papers, Box 9, Letterpress book 11, Archives of the Pierpont Morgan Library, NY, Mar. 12, 1913.

6. Forbes, *Morgan Jr.,* 70.

7. United States Congress, House, Committee on Banking and Currency 1912, https://www.loc.gov/item/13001206, 5.

8. Chernow, *House of Morgan,* 48.

9. Chernow, *House of Morgan,* 48.

10. "Soup and Rome Sun Expected to Restore Morgan," *St. Louis Post-Dispatch,* Mar. 15, 1913, 3.

11. Forbes, *Morgan Jr.,* 72.

12. "J. P. Morgan Dies after Hard Fight in Rome Inn," *San Francisco Examiner,* Apr. 1, 1913, 1.

13. J. P. Morgan Jr. Papers, Box 9, Letterpress book 11, Archives of the Pierpont Morgan Library, NY, Mar. 18, 1913.

14. "J. P. Morgan, King of Finance, Dies in Rome," *Asbury Park (NJ) Evening Press,* Mar. 31, 1913, 1.

15. "J. P. Morgan, World's Greatest Power in Finance Marts, Dead," *San Francisco Call,* Apr. 1, 1913, 1.

16. "Death of J. P. Morgan No Surprise to Wall Street," *Wall Street Journal,* Apr. 1, 1913, 6.

17. "Roosevelt's Tribute to Morgan's Memory," *Hartford Courant,* Apr. 11, 1913, 8.

18. *The Literary Digest,* vol. 46, p. 812, https://archive.org/details/literarydigest-46newy/page/812/mode/2up.

19. Lindbergh, *Banking,* 27.

20. Lindbergh, *Banking,* 27.

21. Strouse, *Morgan,* 531.

22. "As to the Successor of J. P. Morgan," *Boston Daily Globe,* Apr. 1, 1913, 2.

23. "He Controlled Nine Billions," *Wichita Eagle,* Apr. 1, 1913, 4.

24. Forbes, *Morgan Jr.,* 75.

25. *Boston Evening Transcript,* Mar. 31, 1913, 4.

26. Chernow, *House of Morgan,* 161.

27. Cover of *Time Magazine,* Sept. 24, 1923; Feb. 23, 1929; Jan. 20, 1936.

16. RATIONAL AND MEASURED

1. Frank Holt, "Goethe Satyros, Shakespeare und die Bibel" (PhD diss., Cornell, 1914), Cornell University Library Archives.

2. Envious peoples everywhere: "Historical Firearms," https://www.historical-firearms.info/post/93437409959/kaiser-wilhelms-balcony-speeches-on-the-31st.

3. "Wilson Appeals to Americans for Neutrality," *Times (NY) Union,* Aug. 18, 1914, 1.

4. *The Fatherland,* vol. 1, Aug. 1914–Feb. 1915, https://www.google.com/books/edition/The_Fatherland/_IZDAAAAYAAJ?hl=en&gbpv=1&dq=Russia+wants+Constantinople,+France+wants+revenge,+and+England+wants+Germanys+commerce.+On+one+morning+nine+German+ships+were+sunk+with+all+onboard.&pg=PA2&printsec=frontcover.

5. "Morgan & Company Sound U. S. on French Loan," *New York Sun,* Aug. 15, 1914, 5.

6. "American Press Criticized for Its Treatment of War," *Ithaca Journal,* Sept. 23, 1914, 8.

7. Hugo Musterberg, *The War and America* (New York: D. Appleton & Company, 1914), 7.

8. Musterberg, *War and America*, 7.

9. "A Reply to Harvard's President Emeritus," *New York Times*, Sept. 7, 1914, 6.

10. "A Reply to Harvard's President Emeritus."

11. "Enthusiastic Demonstrations Show Raging War Spirit of Foreigners in New York City," *Pittsburg Press*, Aug. 9, 1914, 50.

12. "Germans Here Rush to Arms," *Chicago Tribune*, Aug. 4, 1914, 5.

13. "German Atrocities Fiction, So Far as Tribune Men in Belgium Can Find," *Chicago Tribune*, Sept. 17, 1914, 1.

14. "Staats-Zeitung's Account of Proposed French Loan," *New York Times*, Aug. 15, 1914, 10.

15. "Financiers Confer," *Cincinnati Enquirer*, July 31, 1914, 2.

17. A LONG LETTER

1. Daniel M. Smith, "Robert Lansing and the Formulation of American Neutrality Policies, 1914–1915," *The Mississippi Valley Historical Review* 43, no. 1 (1956): 62.

2. "Public Circular Issued by the Secretary of State, Oct. 15, 1914, regarding neutrality and trade in contraband," https://history.state.gov/historicaldocuments/frus1914Supp/pg_573; https://www.loc.gov/resource/rbpe.24002900/?st=text (with corrected date).

3. "Pro German Letter by Holt," *New York Times*, July 6, 1915, 5.

18. LET WELL ENOUGH ALONE

1. Erich Muenter, Harvard College Library, June 6, 1906.

2. "Knew Holt, Let Him Alone," *Daily Review* (Towanda, PA), July 7, 1915, 1.

3. "Knew Holt, Let Him Alone."

4. "Knew Holt, Let Him Alone."

5. "Knew Holt, Let Him Alone."

6. Thomas J. Tunney, *Throttled: The Detection of the German and Anarchist Bomb Plotters in the United States* (Boston: Small, Maynard & Company, 1919), 12.

7. Southern Methodist University Library Archives, Frank Holt.

8. "Faculty List Announced," *Fort Worth-Record Telegram*, Apr. 13, 1915, 4.

9. "J. P. Morgan Home, Silent on Finance," *New York Times*, May 10, 1915, 11.

10. *The Nereide*, 13 US 388, 3 L. Ed. 769 (1815).

19. MILLS HOTEL

1. "A Decent Bed and with Luck a Dry Towel," *New York Times*, Jan. 30, 2011, RE MB 6.

2. "How Sinking of *Lusitania* is regarded in the press," *Chicago Daily Tribune*, May 9, 1915, 2.

20. MR. TOTTEN

1. "F. Holt Was Wife Slayer," *Courier-Journal* (Louisville, KY), July 8, 1915, 2.
2. "F. Holt Was Wife Slayer."
3. "Dynamite Buyer Had Holt's Alias," *New York Times,* July 6, 1915, 4.

21. JULY 1

1. "Morgan's Assailant Is Baffled in Attempt to Open an Artery in Arm," *Akron Beacon Journal,* July 6, 1915, 1.
2. "Morgan's Assailant."

22. JULY 2

1. "Holt Kills Himself in Jail," *New York Tribune,* July 7, 1915, 2.
2. "Set an Infernal Machine," *New York Times,* July 4, 1914, 1.

23. JULY 3

1. "J. P. Morgan Shot by Teacher of German Who Put Dynamite Bomb in the Capitol," *Sun,* July 4, 1915, 2.
2. "J. P. Morgan Shot by Teacher of German."
3. "J. P. Morgan Shot by Pro German Fanatic Who Set Senate Bomb, Condition Good," *New York Tribune,* July 4, 1915, 2.
4. "Intruder Has Dynamite," *New York Times,* July 4, 1915, 1.
5. "Intruder Has Dynamite."
6. "Intruder Has Dynamite."
7. "Intruder Has Dynamite."
8. "Intruder Has Dynamite."
9. "Intruder Has Dynamite."
10. "Intruder Has Dynamite."
11. "Intruder Has Dynamite."
12. "Morgan Office Allay Disquiet," *Chicago Daily Tribune,* July 4, 1915, 3.
13. "Man Who Shot J. P. Morgan Confesses He Set off Dynamite Bomb in Capitol," *Boston Daily Globe,* July 4, 1915, 1.
14. "Deplorable Act of Crazed Man," *New York Tribune,* July 4, 1915, 3.
15. "Holt Arraigned for Assault on Morgan," *Nashville Tennessean and the Nashville American,* July 4, 1915, 12A.
16. *Gideon v. Wainwright,* 372 US 335 (1963).
17. "Shot J. P Morgan," *Kansas City Star,* July 3, 1915, 3.
18. "Intruder Has Dynamite," *New York Times,* July 4, 1915, 1.
19. "Intruder Has Dynamite," *New York Times,* July 4, 1915, 1.

20. "Supposed Crank Attempts Life of J. P. Morgan at Glen Cove by United Press," *Plainfield (NJ) Courier-News,* July 3, 1915, 1.

21. "Supposed Crank Attempts Life of J. P. Morgan."

22. "Holt, Morgan's Assailant Tells about Himself," *Brooklyn Daily Eagle,* July 4, 1915, 4.

23. "Holt, Morgan's Assailant Tells about Himself."

24. "Holt, Morgan's Assailant Tells about Himself."

25. "Holt, Morgan's Assailant Tells about Himself."

26. "Holt, Morgan's Assailant Tells about Himself."

27. "Holt, Morgan's Assailant Tells about Himself."

28. "Holt, Morgan's Assailant Tells about Himself."

29. "Holt, Morgan's Assailant Tells about Himself."

30. "Crank Shoots J. P. Morgan," *Fort Worth Star-Telegram,* July 3, 1915, 1.

31. "Friends Think Holt Is Insane," *Chicago Tribune,* July 4, 1915, 3.

32. "Mental Aberration," *Cincinnati Enquirer,* July 4, 1915, 2.

33. "Mental Aberration."

34. "Mental Aberration."

35. "Holt Native Texan; His Wife in Dallas," *Brooklyn Daily Eagle,* July 4, 1915, 4.

36. "Wife Unable to Clear Mystery of Holt's Life," *St. Louis Dispatch,* July 5, 1915, 2.

37. "Holt Is Insane, Say Relatives of Dallas, Tex," *Tulsa World,* July 4, 1915, 1.

38. "Frank Holt Believed with Tolstoi; Peace to All Mankind," *Dallas Daily Times Herald,* July 5, 1915, 2.

39. "Pullman in New York Has Talk with Holt on Bomb Outrage Here," *Evening Star,* July 4, 1915, 8.

40. "Explosion Damages Room at Capitol; Police without a Clue," *Evening Star,* July 3, 1915, 2.

41. "Explosion Damages Room at Capitol."

42. Tunney, *Throttled,* 194.

43. Tunney, *Throttled,* 194.

44. "Pullman in New York Has Talk with Holt on Bomb Outrage Here," *Evening Star* (Washington, DC), 8.

45. "Morgan Estate an Armed Camp," *New York Times,* July 4, 1915, 1.

46. "Bankers Wife Rescues Him at Own Peril," *Chicago Daily Tribune,* July 4, 1915, 1.

47. "Holt Planned to Kill Family with Dynamite," *Chicago Daily Tribune,* July 5, 1915, 4.

48. "Holt Planned to Kill Family."

49. Undated letter, no names, Glen Cove Public Library Archives, Glen Cove, NY.

50. Tunney, *Throttled,* 192.

51. "Holt, Morgan's Assailant Tells about Himself."

52. "Intruder Has Dynamite."

53. "Tried to End Arms Exports, Not Harm Morgan Says Holt," *Washington Times,* July 4, 1915, 4.

54. "Tried to End Arms Exports."

55. "Tried to End Arms Exports."

56. "Tried to End Arms Exports."
57. "Tried to End Arms Exports."
58. "Tried to End Arms Exports."
59. "Tried to End Arms Exports."
60. "Tried to End Arms Exports."
61. "Tried to End Arms Exports."
62. "Tried to End Arms Exports."
63. "Tried to End Arms Exports."
64. "Tried to End Arms Exports."
65. "Tried to End Arms Exports."
66. "Tried to End Arms Exports."
67. "Holt Makes Statement," *Elmira Star Gazette,* July 3, 1915, 5.
68. "Tried to End Arms Exports."
69. Tunney, *Throttled,* 192.
70. Tunney, *Throttled.*
71. Tunney, *Throttled.*
72. Tunney, *Throttled.*
73. Tunney, *Throttled.*
74. "J. P. Morgan Shot by Same Man That Tried to Blow up Capitol," *Rochester Democrat and Chronicle,* July 4, 1915, 3.
75. "J. P. Morgan Shot by Same Man."
76. Tunney, *Throttled.*
77. Tunney, *Throttled.*
78. Tunney, *Throttled.*
79. Tunney, *Throttled.*
80. Tunney, *Throttled.*
81. Tunney, *Throttled.*
82. Tunney, *Throttled.*
83. Tunney, *Throttled.*
84. Tunney, *Throttled.*
85. Tunney, *Throttled.*
86. "Pullman in New York Has Talk with Holt on Bomb Outrage Here," *Sunday Star,* (Washington, DC), July 4, 1915, part I, 8.
87. "Man Who Shot Morgan Also Placed Bomb," *Atlanta Constitution,* July 4, 1915, 1.
88. Tunney, *Throttled.*
89. Tunney, *Throttled.*
90. "Find Letter to the Kaiser Hidden in Holt's Suitcase," *Boston Globe,* July 5, 1915, 2.
91. "Find Letter to the Kaiser."

24. JULY 4

1. "J. P. Morgan Shot by the Man Who Set the Capitol Bomb," *Madison Journal* (Tallulah, LA), July 10, 1915, 1.

2. “Man Who Shot J. P. Morgan Confesses He Set off Dynamite Bomb in Capitol,” *Boston Daily Globe,* July 4, 1915, 1.

3. “Holt Reveals Plan to Take Morgan Family as Arms Embargo Hostages,” *New York Tribune,* July 5, 1915, 1.

4. “Holt Reveals Plan.”

5. “Holt Reveals Plan.”

6. *Dallas Daily Times Herald,* July 4, 1915, 1.

7. “Family of Holt Stunned by His Deeds,” *Gazette Time* (Pittsburg, PA), July 4, 1915, 2.

8. “Holt’s Past Dark to Wife,” *New York Times,* July 6, 1915, 4.

9. *Dallas Daily Times Herald,* July 4, 1915, 1.

10. “Poem Written by Frank Holt Shows His Morbid Tendency,” *Ithaca Journal,* July 7, 1915, 1.

11. “No Indication in Holt’s Papers That He Had an Accomplice,” *St. Louis Post-Dispatch,* July 9, 1915, 2.

12. “I’m the Goat: Holt’s Keeper,” *Chicago Tribune,* July 9, 1915, 3.

13. “Find Muenter Case Clippings in Holt’s Quarters in Ithaca,” *Brooklyn Daily Eagle,* July 8, 1915, 2.

14. “Minnehaha Safe at Halifax; Fire Investigation on,” *Asbury Park Evening Press,* July 9, 1915, 6.

15. “Morgan Insists That Yachts Race,” *New York Times,* July 4, 1915, S1.

16. “Holt Case,” *Buffalo Evening Times,* July 6, 1915, 2.

25. JULY 5

1. “Holt Frenzied over Failure of His Mission,” *Chicago Tribune,* July 6, 1915, 3.

2. “Holt Frenzied over Failure.”

3. “Holt Frenzied over Failure.”

4. “Is Frank Holt Erich Muenter?,” *Ft. Wayne News,* July 5, 1915, 1.

5. “Holt Insane Morgan out Soon,” *New York Tribune,* July 6, 1915, 1.

6. “Holt Kills Himself in Jail,” *New York Tribune,* July 7, 1915, 1.

7. Tunney, *Throttled,* 205.

8. “Found Holt Scarred as Was Dr. Muenter,” *New York Times,* July 7, 1915, 2.

9. “Holt Laughs at Story That He Is Muenter,” *Washington Times,* July 5, 1915, 2.

10. “Sought Hostages Holt Now Insists,” *New York Times,* July 5, 1915, 2.

11. “Holt Insane, Morgan out Soon,” *New York Tribune,* July 6, 1915, 1.

12. “Explosion Damages Room at Capitol; Police without a Clue,” *Evening Star,* July 3, 1915.

13. US Senate, Subcommittee on Appropriations, General Deficiency Bill, Aug. 30, 1916, https://www.google.com/books/edition/General_Deficiency_Bill_1916/3VQuAAAAMAAJ?hl=en&gbpv=1&dq=1916+HR+17645+Appropriations+committee&pg=PA3&printsec=frontcover.

14. “Saved Spring-Rice from Hold-Up Men,” *New York Times,* July 13, 1915, 1.

15. Tunney, *Throttled,* 208.
16. Tunney, *Throttled,* 208.
17. *Chicago Daily Tribune,* July 5, 1915, 1.
18. "'Holt' Is Her Brother Muenter's Sisters Declare," *New York Tribune,* July 6, 1915, 1.
19. "Muenter Indictment for Murder Stolen," *New York Times,* July 6, 1915, 5.
20. "Where Muenter Got Money Puzzles His People in Dallas," *Brooklyn Daily Eagle,* July 8, 1915, 2.

26. JULY 6

1. "Holt Attempts Suicide in Cell; Morgan 'Fine,'" *Times Union* (Albany, NY), July 6, 1915, 1.
2. "Suicide Attempt Is Made by Frank Holt," *Moline Daily Dispatch,* July 6, 1915, 5.
3. "Body Scars May Prove Identity," *Elmira-Star Gazette,* July 6, 1915, 2.
4. "Holt Is Muenter Asserts Teacher," *South Bend Tribune,* July 6, 1915, 3.
5. "Critics Silence Prof. Gould," *New York Times,* July 8, 1915, 2.
6. "Krembs Going to Prosecute Holt-Muenter," *Chicago Daily Tribune,* July 6, 1915, 1.
7. "Holt Not Popular at Emory and Henry," *Richmond Times-Dispatch,* July 6, 1915, 2.
8. "Holt Will Not Clear Mystery about Identity," *Austin American,* July 6, 1915, 1.
9. "Sure Holt Was Muenter," *New York Times,* July 7, 1915, 3.
10. *Dallas Daily Times Herald,* July 6, 1915, 1.
11. "Father-in-law Does Not Believe He Was Muenter," *Houston Post,* July 7, 1915, 1.
12. "Mrs. Holt in Most Serious Condition," *Austin American,* July 7, 1915, 3.
13. US Senate, Subcommittee on Appropriations, General Deficiency Bill, Aug. 30, 1916, https://www.google.com/books/edition/General_Deficiency_Bill_1916/3VQuAAAAMAAJ?hl=en&gbpv=1&dq=1916+HR+17645+Appropriations+committee&pg=PA3&printsec=frontcover.
14. "Muenter's Last Letter Home," *New York Times,* July 8, 1915, 2.
15. "Holt's Suicides: Mystery in Act," *Post-Star* (Glens Falls, NY), July 7, 1915, 1.
16. "134 Sticks of Dynamite Is Found in a House in New York," *Washington Post,* July 7, 1915, 2.
17. Tunney, *Throttled,* 210.

27. JULY 7

1. "Holt Wrote to His Wife about Blowing up Ships," *Waco Times-Herald,* July 7, 1915, 1.
2. "Holts Wife Not Told of His Death on Advice of Family Physician," *Washington Post,* July 7, 1915, 2.

3. "Autopsy Fails to Clear up Cause of Death," *Hartford Courant,* July 7, 1915, 11.

4. "Exposer of Holt Tells Story of His Exposure," *Chicago Tribune,* July 7, 1915, 2.

5. "Muenter's Sisters Sure Holt Is Erich," *New York Sun,* July 6, 1915, 2.

6. "Professor Kept Muenter Secret Knew Him Well," *Star-Gazette* (Elmira, NY), July 8, 1915, 2.

7. "Professor Kept Muenter Secret."

8. "Professor Kept Muenter Secret."

9. "Holt Wrote to His Wife about Blowing up Ships."

10. "Would Finish Holt's Work," *Monroe (LA) News-Star,* July 12, 1915, 1

28. FRANK HOLT

1. *In the Matter of the Inquisition as to the Death of Frank Holt,* Justice's Court, Town of Hempstead, Nassau County, NY, July 27, 1915, 12.

2. "Sang 'Lead Kindly Light' at Funeral of Frank Holt Sunday Evening—Few Were Present," *Dallas Daily Times Herald,* July 12, 1915, 4.

EPILOGUE

1. "J. P. Morgan Threatened," *Brooklyn Daily Eagle,* Feb. 1, 1912, 1.

2. Forbes, *Morgan Jr.,* 100.

3. Chernow, *House of Morgan,* 373.

4. Susie Pak, *Gentleman's Banker, The World of J. P. Morgan* (Cambridge, MA: Harvard Univ. Press, 2013), 147.

5. Forbes, *Morgan Jr.,* 103.

6. Robert M. Pennoyer, *As It Was, a Memoir* (Burlington, VT: Prospecta Press, 2015),

7. "Wall Street Explosion Kills 30, Injures 300," *New York Times,* Sept. 17, 1920, 1.

8. Chernow, House of Morgan, 262.

9. "Mrs. J. P. Morgan Dies at Glen Cove Home; In a Coma Two Months," *New York Times,* Aug. 15, 1925, 1.

10. "Morgan Memorial Park at Glen Cove Dedicated," *New York Herald Tribune,* July 17, 1932, 9.

11. Chernow, *House of Morgan,* 593.

12. "Notables Receive Princeton Degrees," *New York Times,* June 19, 1929, 26.

13. Chernow, House of Morgan, 265.

14. United States Senate, https://www.senate.gov/about/powers-procedures/investigations/pecora.htm#:~:text=On%20March%202%2C%201932%2C%20senators,lending%E2%80%9D%20of%20stocks%20and%20securities.

15. Chernow, *House of Morgan,* 545.

16. Hearings before the Committee on Banking and Currency United States Senate, Seventy-Third Congress, First Session on S.Res. 84, (72d Congress), May

23, 24, 25, 1933, https://fraser.stlouisfed.org/title/stock-exchange-practices-87/hearings-s-res-84-s-res-56–33957/fulltext.

17. "Tax Evasion by Morgan in Legal Stock Dealing Is Now Hunted by Pecora," *New York Times,* June 2, 1933, 1.

18. Forbes, *Morgan Jr.,* 179.

19. Chernow, *House of Morgan,* 519.

20. Pennoyer, *As It Was,* 61.

21. Forbes, *Morgan Jr.,* 117.

22. Forbes, *Morgan Jr.,* 117.

23. Forbes, *Morgan Jr.,* 189.

24. "J. P. Morgan, Financial Titan, Is Dead," *Gazette,* (Cedar Rapids, OH), Mar. 13, 1943, 1.

25. "Head of House of Morgan for 30 Years Disliked Being in Public's Eye and Was Distressed by Midget Who Sat on Lap at Senate Hearing," *St Louis Star-Times,* Mar. 13, 1943, 11

26. Forbes, *Morgan Jr.,* 75.

27. Chernow, *House of Morgan,* 316.

28. Helen Wooddell Crawford, *Newspaper Obituaries 1910–1922, Cherokee County, Texas, Book 2,* Cherokee County Historical Commission, Rusk, TX, 222.

BIBLIOGRAPHY

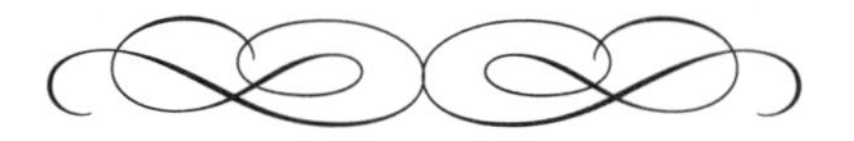

Allen, Frederick Lewis. *The Lords of Creation.* New York: Harper & Brothers, 1935.

———. *The Great Pierpont Morgan.* New York: Dorset Press, 1989.

Baatz, Simon. *The Girl on the Velvet Swing: Sex, Murder, and Madness at the Dawn of the Twentieth Century.* New York: Mulholland Books, 2018.

Blum, Howard. *Dark Invasion.* New York: Crown, 2014.

Bolotin, Norman, and Christine Laing. *The World's Columbian Exposition, The Chicago World's Fair of 1893.* Washington, DC: Preservation Press, 1992.

Brandeis, Louis D. *Other People's Money, and How Bankers Use It.* New York: Frederick A. Stokes Co., 1914.

Brown, Risa. *Polytechnic Days.* Dallas: Alliance Publishing LLC, 2020.

Carosso, Vincent P. *The Morgans Private International Bankers 1854–1913.* Cambridge, MA: Harvard Univ. Press, 1987.

Chernow, Ron. *The House of Morgan: An American Banking Dynasty and the Rise of Modern Finance.* New York: Atlantic Monthly Press, 1990.

Forbes, John Douglas. *J. P. Morgan Jr. 1867—1943.* Charlottesville, VA: Univ. Press of Virginia, 1981.

Gill, Gillian. *Mary Baker Eddy.* Radcliffe Biography Series. Cambridge, MA: Da Capo Press, 1999.

Harbaugh, William Henry. *Lawyer's Lawyer, the life of John W. Davis.* Charlottesville, VA: Univ. of Virginia Press, 1990.

Harkup, Kathryn. *A is for Arsenic: The Poisons of Agatha Christie.* New York: Bloomsbury, 2017.

Heinen Joseph C., and Susan Barton Heinen. *Lost German Chicago Images of America.* Mount Pleasant, SC: Arcadia Publishing, 2009.

Holt, Frank. "Goethe Satyros, Shakespeare und die Bibel." PhD diss., Cornell Univ., 1914. Cornell Univ. Library Archives.

Huber, William R. *George Westinghouse: Powering the World.* Jefferson, NC: McFarland & Company Inc., 2022.

Ismay, Clifford. *Understanding J. Bruce Ismay.* Cheltenham, UK: History Press, 2022.

Jones, John Price. *The German Spy in America.* London: Hutchinson & Co., 1917.

Krembs, Moritz. Diary. Private papers of William MacDonald.

Levinson, Leonard Lewis. *Wall Street: A Pictorial History.* New York: Ziff-Davis Publishing Co., 1961.

Lindberg, Charles August. *Banking and Currency and the Money Trust.* N.p.: C. A. Lindberg, 1913. https://archive.org/details/pdfy-ly2qbyfaWtQyLoqw/mode/2up.

Maguire, Kathleen. *Chicago Then and Now.* London: Pavilion Books, 2015.

Morgan, Joseph. *The Nature of Riches.* Oxford: Univ. of Oxford, 1732. https://ota.bodleian.ox.ac.uk/repository/xmlui/bitstream/handle/20.500.12024/N02986/N02986.html?sequence=5&isAllowed=y.

Muenter, Erich. "Sensation! Scandal! Autopsy Cremation Assfixiation [*sic*]." June 6, 1906. Harvard College Library.

Nightingale, Florence. *Notes on Nursing.* London: Harrison, 1860.

O'Donnell, Edward T. *Ship Ablaze: The Tragedy of the Steamboat General Slocum.* New York: Crown, 2004.

Pak, Susie J. *Gentlemen Bankers, The World of J. P. Morgan.* Cambridge, MA: Harvard Univ. Press, 2013.

Pennoyer, Robert M. *As It Was: A Memoir.* Torrington, CT: Prospecta Press, 2015.

Perino, Michael. *The Hellhound of Wall Street: How Ferdinand Pecora's Investigation of the Great Crash Forever Changed American Finance.* London: Penguin Press, 2010.

Schiff, Warren. "Germans in Mexican Trade and Industry During the Diaz Period." *The Americas* 23, no. 3 (1967): 293.

Strouse, Jean, Morgan. *American Financier.* New York: Random House, 2012.

Tuchman, Barbara W. *The Guns of August.* New York: Presidio Press, 1962.

Tunney, Thomas J. *Throttled: The Detection of German Anarchist Bomb Plotters in the United States.* Boston: Small, Maynard & Company, 1919.

Watson, Katherine. *Poisoned Lives English Poisoners and Their Victims.* New York: Bloomsbury Academic, 2006.

Witthaus, Rudolph August, and Tracy Chatfield Becker. *Medical Jurisprudence, Forensic Medicine and Toxicology.* Vol. 4. New York: William Wood & Company, 1907.

Woolf, Virginia. *Roger Fry: A Biography.* Boston: Mariner Books Classics, 1976.

INDEX

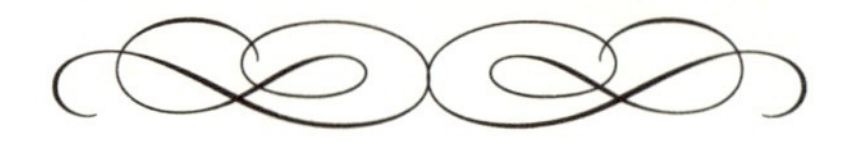